O9-BTZ-888

WITHDRAWN

Out *of the* Shadows

On the Coastal Range
Neil Waldman
Oil on Canvas

Out
of the
Shadows

An Artist's Journey

Neil Waldman

October Meadow
Neil Waldman
Oil on linen

Boyds Mills Press

Acknowledgments

From the earliest imaginings of this project, Kent Brown, publisher, and Clay Winters, president, of Boyds Mills Press have encouraged and supported me as I strove to create the most beautiful book possible. Larry Rosler, editor, understood the underlying possibilities inherent in the manuscript, and guided me towards insights I would never have come to on my own. Alice Cummiskey, managing editor, oversaw the reproduction of the many drawings, paintings, monoprints, and etchings. Tim Gillner, art director, worked closely with me, designing every page in the book. My uncle and cousin, Cal and Jeff Morris, permitted me to sift through my aunt Jeanie's drawings, paintings, and prints, graciously allowing me to borrow all those pieces I chose to include here.

Text copyright © 2006 by Neil Waldman
Artwork copyright © 2006 by Neil Waldman, Bruce Waldman, Bryna Waldman, Maurice Meyer, Jean Morris
All rights reserved

Published by Boyds Mills Press, Inc.
A Highlights Company
815 Church Street
Honesdale, Pennsylvania 18431
Printed in China

Library of Congress Cataloging-in-Publication Data

Waldman, Neil.
  Out of the shadows : an artist's journey / Neil Waldman. — 1st ed.
     p. cm.
  ISBN 1-59078-411-1 (alk. paper)
  1. Waldman, Neil—Childhood and youth—Juvenile literature. 2. Illustrators—United States—Biography—Juvenile literature. 3. Jewish artists—United States—Biography—Juvenile literature. I. Title.

NC975.5.W35A2 2006
741.6'092—dc22   2005021139

First edition, 2006
The text of this book is set in 12-point Baskerville.

Visit our Web site at www.boydsmillspress.com

10 9 8 7 6 5 4 3 2 1

For Aunt Jeanie, Uncle Hick, Brucie, and Bryna,
whose artwork appears on these pages.
And for David,
whose artistry lies within

Jazz Musicians
Bruce Waldman
Etching

Mother and Child
Jean Morris
Woodcut

Chapter One

Finger Paints

᭿I lay beneath the quilts in the midnight bedroom, squeezing the pillow against my ears. I pressed the pillow harder, and harder still, but with no relief. Like razor blades, the hate-filled voices kept piercing the layers of cotton and feathers, slicing into my brain.

Beyond the bedroom door, past the living room and into the kitchen, my parents' screams scalded me from the farthest corner of my grandparents' apartment. Tears flowed into the pillowcase, wet and hot against my cheeks. I felt an invisible cord tightening around my throat, and I struggled not to sob.

Quiet! I've got to be quiet! I can't let them hear me. They can't know I'm not sleeping.

I took in a deep breath, held it as long as I could, and let it out slowly. I inhaled again, and gradually, the cord began to loosen. Opening my eyes, I looked over at my little brother Brucie, sleeping peacefully in his crib.

A night-light projected long shadows from the crib's rails, fanning out across faded yellow walls. I studied the plaster cracks on the ceiling, like black threads of lightning across a crumbling sky. The muffled thunder of my father's voice raged again, and I heard my mother crying.

Oh, Mommy. I want to help you. It's my job to help you. But I'm so scared.

Turning back to the ceiling, I tried to concentrate on the cracks, but it was no use. I couldn't blot out my mother's crying. So I closed my eyes, trying in vain to fall asleep, as my parents' voices kept shattering the stillness. Once again, I pressed the pillow against my ears, but the result was no different than before. I couldn't stop the sounds from coming through the walls.

It seemed like hours before a heavy silence fell over the apartment.

❖

Unable to sleep, I rose from bed, tiptoed down the hallway, and slipped on my shoes and coat. Leaving the front door ajar, I made my way down three flights of unlit stairs, and stepped out onto Daly Avenue. Cold rain pelted my forehead as I watched a group of bearded men in black coats scurrying across the sidewalks and disappearing inside their little synagogue.

Reb Moishe's wagon passed in front of me, piled

high with hats, old coats, and rags. The *clippity-clop clip-pity-clop* of his old mare's hooves echoed loudly on the cobblestones. I followed behind the wagon, and when it turned the corner onto 180th Street, I could see that the marketplace was teeming with people.

A farmer sprinted by with wire cages under his arms, alive with cackling hens. Vendors hauled push-

The Live Chicken Market
Jean Morris
Woodcut

carts overflowing with potatoes, carrots, beets, and turnips. Shlomo the Toothless, our local fishmonger, spread filets of salmon on beds of ice with his young son Menahem. Shmulik the Butcher stood cranking an iron rod, unfurling his tattered green awning in an attempt to protect the slabs of kosher meat from the driving rain.

As I struggled between the bustling bodies, memories of my mother's cries poured into my brain, and the corners of my mouth began to sag. Now my chest was heaving. I pushed past them and began running along the slippery sidewalks of Vyse Avenue.

❖

I don't know how far or how long I ran, but the next thing I knew, I was slipping through the door, creeping into the apartment. I pulled off my soggy shoes, hung my coat in the hall closet, and tiptoed into the kitchen. Lifting a set of finger paints, a tray of cupcake tins, and a stack of paper from the art shelf, I sat at the table and poured paint into the tins, spreading the paper across the tabletop.

Within seconds, my hands were wet with color. First, I smeared the page with crimson. Then, I pushed a streak of orange across the red. Next came yellow, brown, and then purple. My fingers bolted back and forth across fiery oceans of color. Dipping my left hand into the darkest pan, I scraped it across the page. Black paint sprayed from my fingertips, splattering against the kitchen wall.

"We'll have none of that!" My mother's voice sounded from behind me . . . and I froze.

Squeezing a rag in the sink, she quickly wiped the wall clean. Then it was my turn. She led me back to the sink and soaped my face, my neck, my wrists, and my fingers, and rinsed them in warm water. Then she patted me dry and led me down the hall. Reaching into a closet, she pulled out one of her old white shirts.

"This will be yours from now on," she said.

Slipping the huge garment over my shoulders, she began buttoning it down. As she knelt there before me, I glanced into the mirror and grimaced. My hands, legs, and feet had disappeared beneath sleeves and waist that reached to the floor. Now she began rolling up the sleeves . . . until my fingers reappeared.

"There," she said, turning toward the mirror. "That looks perfect. You see, Neilly, real artists have special pieces of clothing that they wear to protect their shirts and pants from the paint. They're called *smocks*. From now on, this will be *your* smock."

Taking my hand, she led me back into the kitchen and sat me down on a chair. Carefully covering a corner of the floor with unfolded newspapers and taping sheets of newspaper to the walls above them, she placed a little table in the corner.

"And real artists," she continued, "have special places where they paint. They're called *studios*. From now on, this is going to be *your* studio. Now you won't have to worry about messing the walls, the floor, or yourself, and you can paint to your heart's delight!"

She placed a box of crayons and a coloring book on the table, along with a stack of oak tag, three cupcake tins, and the set of finger paints.

Can I keep painting right now?

"Of course you can," she answered. "You can paint here whenever you like."

Reflections
Neil Waldman
Oil on linen

Chapter Two

The Book

‿∴A s the days blurred into weeks and months, I kept painting and sketching in my new studio. My mother bought me a set of watercolors and a pad of special paper, and I adored them. I usually awoke before everyone else, and I'd sit painting pictures of cowboys on bucking broncos, cloud-covered mountain peaks, and anything else that floated into my mind.

Then, on a snowy December morning, my mom said that Brucie had asked if he could join me.

I thought about it for a minute.

It's prob'ly okay . . . so long as he doesn't mess up my studio.

"I'll make sure that he doesn't," she said, smiling.

Winter
Bryna Waldman
Watercolor

Bringing a second chair in from one of the bedrooms, she placed it next to mine. In a matter of seconds, Brucie was scribbling away.

❖

Our mom started plastering the walls, the windows, and even the doors of the apartment with our artwork: bold sunscapes rendered in red, yellow, and blue finger paint; portraits crafted with crayons, shoe polish, and glitter; and sculptures constructed with papier-mâché, tin foil, and Popsicle sticks.

And as the frosty winter days melted into spring, our paintings grew bigger and brighter . . . and so did we!

On a sunny morning in May, our mom started carrying armloads of art supplies out of the kitchen and into the living room. Unfurling a giant roll of paper, and spreading it across the living room floor, she turned on the record player and called to Brucie and me.

"Come see your new studio," she said as we stepped into the room.

Brucie and I just stood there with our eyes widening and our mouths dropping open.

Is this really gonna be our studio?

"Yes," she said, nodding. "It most certainly is. The kitchen has gotten much too small for the two of you."

But what're we gonna do for a living room?

"You let me worry about that."

In a flash, the two of us flopped down onto the floor and got right to work.

With Beethoven and Bach wafting into our ears, Brucie and I spent the rest of that day basking in the sunshine of our new studio, surrounded by a swirling sea of watercolors, pencils, crayons, and cupcakes. And over the coming weeks and months, we would remain there on the floor, concocting, creating, inventing, imagining . . . and dreaming.

❖

The biggest wall in the living room was filled with bookshelves. Starting about a foot above the floor, the highest shelf reached almost to the ceiling. Nearly every shelf was packed solid with books.

Brucie and I knew that those books were our family's most treasured possessions, and that among them was one book more valuable than all of the others. It remained far beyond our reach, like a beacon shining down into our world from the highest shelf. Sitting alone up there, it was the only object in the apartment that we weren't allowed to touch.

One afternoon, when our mom went to fetch Brucie after a play-date at a friend's apartment, I was left alone for a few minutes. I looked up at the book, and an idea floated into my mind. I quickly grabbed a chair, pushed it against the shelves, and climbed up onto it. Standing on tiptoe, I stretched up as far as I could, but the book was just too high.

It seemed to me that the only times the book wasn't up there on its shelf, my mom had it with her.

I remember once, walking through the kitchen. There was my mom, busy washing dishes . . . and sitting on the countertop next to the sink was the book.

On another occasion, Brucie and I were sculpting with clay. Our mom walked into the living room, took the book down from its shelf, and disappeared into her bedroom, closing the door behind her.

I only got to see her open it once.

Brucie and I were playing with pipe cleaners on the living room floor, when she walked in, took the book down from its shelf, sat on the couch, and started leafing through it. As she flipped from page to page, I noticed a smile spreading across her face.

There must be something amazing in that book that can make my mom so happy.

But I'd never gotten to see what that something was. Neither had Brucie . . . or our cousins . . . our friends . . . or anyone else.

Until one afternoon.

I was walking down the hallway, through the living room, and into the kitchen. There ahead of me, sitting all by itself on the kitchen table, was . . . the book.

T h e   b o o k !

I quickly scanned the apartment. There wasn't anybody else around. I checked the rooms again, and my eyes returned to the kitchen table.

Amazing! I've never seen the book . . . alone . . . and within reach!

I stood motionless for an eternity of heartbeats.

Then suddenly, my feet were moving.

Approaching the table on tiptoe, I lifted myself onto a chair, reached up, and touched the book. I felt its soft velvety cover, inhaled its rich musty smell, studied the shiny golden letters of its title: unreadable letters in a strange and unfamiliar alphabet.

And then . . . I reached over with my left hand . . . and opened it.

Between my hands on broad pages of the purest white were two landscapes whose colors seemed to be glowing, spinning, sparkling. I gazed into the skies of the landscape on the right-hand page. A torrent of blue, turquoise, and violet brushstrokes swirled around a shimmering orange sun.

My God! I've never seen so many colors in the skies before.

I jumped off the chair, ran to the window, and peered out at an endless sea of gray-bellied clouds scraping the soot-stained rooftops of the Bronx.

Then I quickly returned to the book.

I have to know more about these colors . . . but I can't ask Mommy . . . She'll kill me if she finds out that I touched her book.

As I sat there, lost in those amazing landscapes, my curiosity began to grow, like a small seed sprouting in my chest, and I wondered,

How could a human being have created colors this beautiful? . . . And who could that person be . . . and when did he or she paint it . . . and where did he or she come from?

Then . . . a thought crept into my mind.

In all the world, there's one person who can answer these questions.

I took in a deep breath, and left the kitchen.

I found her straightening up in Grandma and Grandpa's bedroom. Approaching her from behind, I reached up and tugged at her skirt. She turned toward me, and I lowered my eyes, trying to speak while staring at my shoelaces.

M o m m y . . . I . . . o p e n e d y o u r b o o k .

To my surprise (and relief), she looked down at me and smiled, took my hand, and led me back into the kitchen. Sitting on the chair, she placed me on her lap.

We both sat there for a long time, gazing at the paintings.

Then she asked, "Well, what do you think?"

Please, Mommy. Please tell me everything about the colors.

She was quiet for a while, and then she started speaking.

"These colors were created with a special kind of paint that's made from oil."

That seemed really strange to me.

There was only one kind of oil I knew about: the stuff she mixed with vinegar and poured over salad.

Next, she said something almost as strange.

"They're not painted on paper, but on the kind of cloth that the sails of ships are made of. It's called canvas."

Now she looked away from the book, raised her eyebrows, and spoke again.

The House at Auvers (from Vincent van Gogh)
Neil Waldman
Oil on linen

"The name of the man who painted them is Vincent van Gogh."

❖

As I sat there, basking in the glow of those amazing landscapes, my mother kept speaking. She spoke about ideas, new ideas that were strange and unfamiliar . . . things she called "purity of pigment," "complementary color," and "Post-Impressionism."

When she finished speaking, I was afraid she'd put the book back up on the shelf, so I asked,

Can I keep looking at the book?

Her answer has remained etched in my memory for more than half a century. (Later that day, I wrote it down in one of my journals . . . so I still remember every word.)

"You may look at this book whenever you like," she began, "if you'll make me one promise. You see, Grandma Kate brought this book with her from Russia many years ago. It's my most prized possession in the whole world. And if you're to use it, you must treat it with the respect it deserves. You must promise me that every time you touch it, you'll pretend that it's a priceless piece of crystal that must be treated with the greatest of care."

Of course I gave her my word.

I spent the rest of that afternoon with the book, and as I leafed through its sacred pages, I discovered painting after painting that lifted me into worlds of wonder and mystery. From within the book's pages, Vincent van Gogh's hands seemed to reach out, take hold of my shoulders, and carry me into his paintings.

Our apartment vanished.

I found myself floating between rows of spiraling cypress trees, sailing through fields of waving grasses. I passed chartreuse farmhouses with baby-blue roofs and purple shutters . . . into meadows speckled with red and yellow poppies, while high above me swirling skies sparkled in ultramarine splendor.

By dinnertime, I decided that Vincent van Gogh was my hero. I wanted to grow up to be an artist just like him, and I knew that if I worked really hard, someday some of my own paintings just might be included in a book like this.

❖

Our family had come to the Bronx from Russia and Galicia just after the turn of the last century.

Between Vyse and Daly Avenues, 180th Street and Bronx Park South, lived one grandma, two grandpas, three tantas, four uncles, dozens of cousins, and scores of friends from the Old Country.

It seemed to me that everyone in the world lived in our neighborhood.

Weekends and holidays were spent gathering in one another's apartments, and at those gatherings, the grown-ups would always approach the children with the same disturbing questions: "You are our family's first generations born in freedom. So what are you going to do with it? What are you going to be when you grow up?"

I'd never considered the future, let alone imagined what it'd be like to be a grown-up. And so the questions always made me uncomfortable. But it wasn't like that with the others. When they asked my cousin Jefferson (note that he wasn't named Geof or Jeffrey), he'd smile and say, "I'm gonna grow up to be a fire engine." And Eddie Weiner, our four-year-old neighbor from the second floor, always lay in waiting for the questions with, "I'm going to grow up to be a tiger!" Cousin Franklin always proclaimed that he was going to be a lawyer. And little Hymie Schnepps was already campaigning to become the Assistant Vice President of the Bronx.

But not me. When grown-ups approached, I'd lower my eyes and speak in an embarrassed whisper.

I'm sorry. I just don't know.

But now, the landscape of my inner world had begun to change. Vincent van Gogh stood there, shining in my dreams, carrying me upon his brushstrokes into a land of suddenly uncovered canvases.

And so, as Grandma Gussie approached me with that familiar look etched on her face, my body tensed. For I had become a lion, and as the graying gazelle drew near, I readied to pounce.

"So, Mister Neilly," she said sarcastically, pinching my cheek. "Have you finally decided what you're going to be, here in this golden land?"

Yes. I am going to be an artist.

I could see by the way she grinned and patted me on the head that she thought that that was a cute thing for a little kid to say. It was clear that she didn't take me seriously. *But I didn't care!* You see, I knew that deep down inside something really had changed. I *was* going to grow up to be an artist, just like Vincent van Gogh.

Meyer Waldman
Jean Morris
Oil on canvas

Chapter Three

Grandpa

ᔛ**D**uring the oppressive afternoons of August, Brucie and I would climb through the kitchen window onto the second-floor fire escape. We'd sit there for hours with crayons and sketchpads, while fleeting breezes tickled our foreheads like invisible ostrich feathers from the heavens.

Then the scorching sun would sink behind the rooftops, darkening the alleyways beneath us, shading the crisscrossing clotheslines strung from fire escape to fire escape. Then Grandma Gussie would call us all to dinner. Brucie and I would crawl in through the window, and sit with our parents, tantas, uncles, and cousins in the unlit kitchen, with sweat dripping into our borscht.

It was a major event in our family's history when our father came home one August evening with an electric fan under his arm. The entire family soon congregated around it, and it seemed to me that no one budged until Yom Kippur.

⋰❖⋱

That October, the four of us moved around the corner to our own apartment at 900 Bronx Park South. It was a really fancy building, complete with a lobby, a marble paver on the lobby's bottom step, and an elevator. Our father called 900 "The Pride of the Bronx."

Abe
Bruce Waldman
Etching

We celebrated that first evening with a dinner of potato latkes and sour cream, just for the four of us, and then Brucie and I returned happily to our new bedroom. I sat at the window for hours, gazing out across the brick and concrete world of the East Bronx. I watched smoke rising from the chimney stacks of the Wonder Bread factory. I listened to the rumble of an elevated subway train, loud on the trestles as it passed between the buildings. Then I looked past the benches that lined the sidewalks across the street, to the iron fence that stood between the city and the zoo.

That fence seemed to separate two worlds.

On the near side lay the man-made world: a world of cobblestones, clanking streetcars, and endless rows of buildings. On the far side lay a quieter world: a world of swaying treetops, lawns, and meadows. And as I gazed out across that world, it whispered to me, bringing a smile to my lips and a joy to my heart. For I knew that it was a miracle that we now lived across the street from such a green and beautiful place.

❖

Early the next morning, there was a knocking at the door, and Grandpa Meyer entered our apartment.

"So . . . how would you like to go to the zoo?" he asked me in gentle Yiddish-English.

Grandpa took my hand and led me out onto the sidewalk, past groups of women rocking baby carriages, as they sat shmoozing on the benches that lined Bronx Park South.

We turned a corner and entered the zoo.

"Before we start our adventure," Grandpa said, "I want to show you my secret place."

He led me over a little fence, across a field, and into a grove of tall pine trees.

"So . . . this is it," Grandpa said, "the most beautiful place in the Bronx. Lie down right here. I think you will like the view."

I lay down on my back, resting my head on a pillow of pine needles.

I stared up into the branches and the blue sky beyond. The clatter of the trolley tracks hushed. The songs of the marketplace faded. The apartment houses vanished.

As I looked about me in every direction, I reveled in the realization that for the first time in my life, I'd come upon a place where I could see no buildings, no vehicles, no man-made objects of any kind.

Thank you, Grandpa.

Grandpa Meyer smiled and gently touched my cheek.

After a long while we got up, brushed ourselves off, and started walking along the zoo's forested pathways. We came to a shady place where the path was enveloped in green darkness.

"Have a looky over there," Grandpa said, pointing to the right.

All I could see was trees.

He knelt down so that I could look past his arm, hand, and pointing finger.

What is it, Grandpa?

"Do you see that light-green place between those branches?"

Just beyond the forest, I could make out a meadow, and across the meadow, I could see a herd of dark-brown animals.

What are they?

"Boo-fallows. You know, like in the cowboy pictures."

You mean real buffalo?

"Yes, actually," Grandpa nodded. "Real boo-fallows!"

As we stood there, the herd started drifting toward us, munching on the grasses of the meadow. There were all sizes, from the huge male with his thick black mane to the three small calves who seemed to be playing tag as they scampered around the slow-moving adults.

Just then a man and a boy walked up behind us.

"There they are, son," the man said. "When you go to school tomorrow, you can tell your teacher you've seen 'The Mother Herd.'"

I waited until they left, and then I turned to Grandpa Meyer.

What does that mean, Grandpa? The Mother Herd?

"I dunno," he said.

The Mother Herd.

That evening, I wrote those three words down in one of my journals, etching them forever in my memory.

Forty-five years later, I was speaking with a children's librarian at a library near my home.

"When I was a little girl," she said, "I used to hear that those buffalo were called 'The Mother Herd', too. And I don't know what it means either!"

Together, we searched the library's shelves, and discovered that an organization called the American Bison Society was founded in the Bronx Zoo in 1905.

I made an appointment to visit the zoo's archives, and as I sat there sifting through stacks of old books, magazines, and photographs, I stumbled upon the remarkable story of how fourteen conservationists from the American Bison Society had rescued the buffalo from the brink of extinction a hundred years ago. I read accounts of how the Society had bred buffalo from the "mother herd" in the Bronx Zoo, sending trainloads of the animals to Oklahoma, South Dakota, Nebraska, and Montana.

Then I came upon an article written by a man who had traveled from the Bronx to Oklahoma with the zoo's first shipment of buffalo in 1907. He described placing fifteen animals in metal cages, loading them onto horse-drawn wagons, and transporting the wagons to a waiting train. They traveled by rail to St. Louis and then south to Oklahoma. And when they reached their final destination, they were met by a group of Comanche Indians, whose children had never seen a buffalo!

The account gave me goose bumps.

Right then and there, I decided that I'd have to write the story through the eyes of one of those children. (It would later become a book titled *They Came from the Bronx*.)

I stopped reading and glanced through an archive window to the meadow where that small herd of buffalo still roamed, and I thought about the long-ago conversation with Grandpa Meyer.

Finally, Grandpa, after all these years, I finally know why those "boo-fallows" are called "The Mother Herd!"

❖

Though I didn't know it at the time, Grandpa Meyer had just been fired from his job at the sweatshop on the Lower East Side where he'd worked for three decades. He remained out of work for nearly half a year, and during that time we visited the zoo almost every day.

We formed a secret club that Grandpa named "The Animal Palzers" and pledged that we would always be its only members.

⊰ ❖ ⊱

I'd usually awaken before sunrise, pull on my clothes, gulp down some orange juice and a bowl of corn flakes, and sit doodling with my crayons. Then, at last, I'd hear Grandpa's secret knock. I'd charge to the door and fling it open.

After kissing Mommy and Brucie good-bye, Grandpa and I would prance out across the cobblestones of Bronx Park South. Down the block and around two corners, we'd pass through a copper gate covered with sculpted animals, and enter the magical world of the zoo.

Within seconds, I'd hear the splashing of water and the barking of sea lions. We'd charge up the huge stone stairway that led to their pool. Grandpa would pick me up in his arms, hoist me onto his shoulders, and we'd watch the playful creatures gliding in circles just beneath the surface. Then they'd dive and disappear, slipping into the emerald depths of the pool.

Day after day, Grandpa and I floated through our mornings, listening to lions, chatting with gorillas, feeding goats and guinea pigs, and riding around an oval-shaped track on the backs of elephants.

But then, on a dreaded Monday, Grandpa told me that he'd found a job in a zipper factory in Brooklyn, and I began to cry.

Apes (top), Elephants (bottom)
Bruce Waldman
Etchings

"Don't worry, palzer," he said, wiping my eyes with his handkerchief. "I promise that we will have lots more adventures together."

And as the days drifted into weeks and months, I would come to realize that Grandpa Meyer's promises would always be worth their weight in gold.

The Seder
Jean Morris
Oil on canvas

Chapter Four

First Seder Memory

⤜ That April, Grandma and Grandpa invited every-
one in the family to a Passover Seder in their apart-
ment. Uncle Hick, Aunt Thelma, Uncle Cal, and Aunt
Jeanie would be there, along with my first cousins:
Barbara, Karen, Jefferson, and Jerry. Grandpa's sister,
Tanta Annie Schnepps, was coming, too, along with her
son Bernie and his family, driving all the way from the
Catskill Mountains. Even my father's childhood buddy
Stanley Anderson would be there with Janet, his
fiancée.

After buttoning my white shirt and zipping up a
pair of itchy woolen trousers, I helped Brucie with his
suspenders and straightened his clip-on bow tie. Then
we stepped out into the living room.

"You both look bee-you-tee-ful!" our mom said,

taking our hands, as our father led us into the elevator and out of the building.

I watched the sun setting over the rooftops as Bronx Park South filled with smartly dressed families, heading for Seders around the neighborhood. The sky darkened as the apartment houses cast long blue shadows across the cobblestones. When we turned the corner onto Daly Avenue, I marveled at the golden glow of candles flickering in window after window. We crossed the empty marketplace and climbed to the second-floor landing of Grandma and Grandpa's tenement house.

Turning the key, my father opened the door, and we entered the apartment. Warm and wonderful aromas met my nostrils as I walked into the living room. A long, L-shaped table stretched through the entryway, reaching into the hall and the kitchen.

I gazed across a sea of familiar faces, past white tablecloths, hand-painted wine glasses, china, and silver into Grandpa Meyer's eyes.

"Abie's family's here!" he announced.

Grandpa stood up and walked toward us. After kissing my mom, my dad, and Brucie, he lifted me into his arms and carried me to the table.

"You're sitting with me, palzer!"

Grandpa placed me on the chair next to his, with a cushion and a telephone book on the seat.

"Here," he whispered into my ear. "Take this. They can last a long time, these Seders." He slipped a piece of matzah into my hand.

Then Grandpa cleared his throat, and slowly, the

living room became quiet. He opened his old Hagaddah, and began to read.

"Avadim hayinu . . .

Once we were slaves. . .

b'Mitzrayim.

in the land of Egypt."

Grandpa scanned the table. Turning to me, his gentle gaze met mine, and his gravelly voice filled the room once again.

"Ldor va dor . . .

From generation to generation we must pass this story on."

Now Grandpa paused, looked down, and slipped another piece of matzah under the table. Hiding it between my hands, I lowered my head and began to nibble. Then he returned to his Hagaddah, and we all continued reading together.

"Avadim hayinu . . .

Each of us must imagine
that he himself, she herself was once a slave."

"We must never forget the pain
of the taskmaster's whip."

"We must always remember to treasure
the freedoms we now possess."

"This is the meaning of Passover."

Then Leonard Schnepps, one of my third cousins, asked a question about the Pharaoh, and Grandpa answered slowly and patiently. A bit later, cousin Barbara made an observation about slavery. and that led to a long and heated debate.

Page by page, we discussed every passage in the Hagaddah, and by the time the Seder ended, I was famished. Finally, the feast could begin. We started with Grandma's scrumptious chicken soup with matzah balls. Then we gobbled gefilte fish, devoured chunks of chicken, tsimis and potato kugel, and finished with chocolate-covered macaroons. Then, with happy stomachs, we started singing Passover songs. And we sang and sang . . . until we could sing no more.

❖

After the Seder, Grandpa led me into his bedroom. Closing the door behind us, he lifted me onto the pillows of his bed, and mussed my hair with his big loving hands.

"I have a story for you," he said. "It's the story of the man your father is named after. That man was the father of our people."

I lay my head on Grandpa's belly, and he cleared his throat.

"Long, long ago," he began, "the sky opened and a voice called down into the wilderness. 'I have a gift,' the voice said, 'a sparkling gift, an amazing gift . . . a wisdom gift.' But nobody listened.

"Then one man heard the voice. A man named Avram. 'So . . . what is this?' Avram asked. 'What is this gift, and where is it hiding?'

"'Follow me,' said the voice. 'Come with me now into a land that I will show you. Journey with me and you shall receive the wisdom gift.'

"So Avram followed the voice to the far end of the wilderness, and there he came upon a land flowing with milk and honey.

"'This is the place,' the voice said, 'the green and beautiful land that I have chosen for your children and your children's children.'

"So Avram settled there, and everything soon happened, just as the voice had said it would. And in that land, the voice began singing, and teaching, and giving.

"Avram listened and learned. He studied the wisdom gift until he knew it. And then the voice changed his name to 'Abraham,' which means 'Father of the Nation.'

"Years later, Abraham and his wife, Sarah, began teaching the wisdom gift to their son, Isaac, who grew and taught it to his son, Jacob. And when Jacob grew, he married a woman named Rachel, and together they passed the wisdom gift down to their children.

"After many generations, the wisdom gift was passed on to your Grandpa Henry and Grandma Kate, who taught it to your mama. It was also passed to Grandma Gussie and me. We taught it to your father, and now we will pass it down to you.

"Someday, you will teach it to your own children."

Fifth Avenue Pedestrians
Neil Waldman
Oil on canvas

Chapter Five

In Manhattan

❀I must have fallen asleep as soon as Grandpa's story ended because when I awoke, there were two great lumps beneath the blankets, snoring loudly on both sides of me. I looked up and realized that I'd slept the night in Grandma and Grandpa's bedroom.

Slipping out from between them, I tiptoed down the hallway and found Bertha Fishback sleeping under a pile of quilts on the living-room couch. Uncle Louie and Tanta Esther were nestled on some pillows on the living-room floor. Aunt Jeanie, Uncle Cal, and cousins Jefferson and Jerry were sleeping in the bedroom where Brucie and I used to sleep.

One by one, the relatives awoke, and before long we were all cleaning together. By mid-morning, the apartment looked like it always had. We all sat munching on leftovers and listening to Uncle Louie's tales about the Old Country. Then, after everyone hugged and said good-bye, Grandpa Meyer approached me.

"So . . . how would you like to take a train ride?"

Where to?

"To the city. Your mama tells me that you love looking at pictures. Well . . . there's a museum over there where you can see lots of them. And there's also one more place over there that I've been wanting to show you."

Homage to Seurat
Neil Waldman
Oil on linen

❖

Taking my hand, Grandpa led me out of the apartment, down 180th Street, and up the long stairway to the elevated subway platform. Within minutes we boarded a train, and as it rolled out of the station, Grandpa and I began weaving our way through the crowd of swaying passengers to the front of the lead car. Standing there, with our noses pressed against the front window, we watched as the stores and tenement houses of the Bronx whizzed by beneath us. Then, after a handful of stops, the subway descended into the pitch black underground.

"Come. Let's have a little rest," Grandpa said, and we settled onto a wicker seat as the train sped through the darkness.

Half an hour later, we got off at a place called Wall Street and stepped out into a maze of narrow streets teeming with pedestrians, taxi cabs, and honking cars. The buildings were much taller than any I'd ever seen. So tall, in fact, that when I looked up I could hardly see the sky.

Swept along the sidewalks by the crowd, we crossed a wide avenue, and escaped behind a bench in a tree-shady park. Grandpa lifted me onto his shoulders, and I could see that there were thousands of onlookers crowded in front of us, peering out across a churning sea of gray-green water with white-capped waves that stretched to the horizon. An ocean liner and two freighters sat suspended in the distance, as a ferry boat passed just in front of us, its decks packed with waving people. Far out in the harbor stood an island with the statue of a woman holding a torch above her head.

"I wanted you to see this place first," Grandpa said. "Have a looky over there. Do you see that beautiful lady? She's the Statue of Liberty."

Yes, Grandpa, I sure can see her!

"Well, the first time I got to see that lady, I was a little guy, just like you. She was in a picture in a book in the farmhouse of my grandpa, Zayde Abraham.

"Zayde Abraham told me that the lady lived in a place called America. And he said that this America was a golden land where people didn't hafta worry like we always did, about being hurt or worse because they were Jewish. So I used to sit looking at that picture for hours and hours and hours, and I dreamed about coming here to this America.

"And years later, when *sof sof* (finally) I crossed the ocean with Tanta Annie, we sailed on this broken-down old boat that kept leaking, and *oy vey*, we were so scared. It was three terrible weeks before we got here. The two of us were standing on the deck with hundreds of people, packed solid like a can of sardines. And when we saw that beautiful lady over there, coming right up out of the ocean, well, we all started crying."

After a while, Grandpa wiped his eyes and started speaking again.

"See those buildings over there?"

Just to the right of the statue was an island of red-roofed buildings with green onion domes.

Yes, Grandpa. What's that?

"Ellis Island. Where Grandma Gussie spent her first few months in America."

Gussie's Kitchen
Jean Morris
Etching

Years later I was sitting in Grandma's kitchen. She was standing before the stove preparing potato kreplach (dumplings). As the aroma of frying onions and potatoes filled the air, Grandma piled a plate with steamy kreplach, poured me a glass of milk, and started telling me the story of her childhood.

"I came from a family of poor farmers in a place called Galicia," she began. "The youngest of three children, I was the last to arrive here in America.

"It all started with Uncle Louie," she explained. "Louie was the first to cross the ocean. He found work on a chicken farm in Connecticut, saved his pennies for a year, and sent the money to Uncle Benny. Benny joined Louie on the farm, and six months later I received a package with money for a ticket."

Grandma looked away from me and continued speaking in a quiet voice.

"I was twelve years old when my boat docked at Ellis Island. Somehow, the letter I sent to my brothers, telling the time of my arrival, never got here."

And so she watched and waited behind a chain-link fence as long-lost uncles shed tears of joy, wives embraced waiting husbands, and parents showered their children with kisses.

One by one, the new arrivals were reunited with their families until only Grandma remained. She sat alone in the customs area for six months. Unable to speak English, she couldn't share her fears with the American officials, who were her only companions.

Finally, it was decided that if no one came to claim her, she would be shipped back to Galicia.

In a last desperate effort, a customs official named McCarthy sent Grandma's photo to *The Fovitz*, a local Yiddish newspaper, and on the day before she was to be sent back, Louie and Benny arrived to claim her.

⌒❖⌒

Grandpa Meyer wiped his eyes again and put me down. Taking my hand, he walked me back across the park, and we reentered Wall Street Station.

Twenty minutes later, we were approaching a massive stone building on the sidewalks of Fifth Avenue,

"There she is," Grandpa said. "The Mehter-powlee-tin Museum of Art."

We climbed the biggest, widest staircase I'd ever set eyes on and entered a colossal hallway lined with statues, with giant tapestries decorating the walls. Up another humongous stone staircase and down a corridor, I looked through a doorway and recognized a familiar painting. Stepping up to it, my heart began to pound.

Oh, Grandpa! It's Vincent!

I spun around in amazement.

Every wall was covered with paintings by Vincent van Gogh! There . . . right in front of me, was one of my favorites from my mother's book!— a turquoise, purple, and brown painting of an olive grove on a hill. Next to that one was a dark-green cypress tree with aqua clouds swirling in the skies above it. And next to that one was the painting I recognized from the corridor, a heavily textured self-portrait of Vincent wearing a straw farmer's hat.

I passed from painting to painting, stopping in front of the self-portrait.

Thanks for everything, Vincent.

Then, after a while, I remembered Grandpa. I turned and saw him, standing behind me.

Could we stay here for a while?

"For sure. That's why we came."

Are these really Vincent's real paintings?

"Yeh. I think they should be."

Grandpa
Neil Waldman
Watercolor

They're so much cooler than they are in Mommy's book! You can really see Vincent's brushstrokes . . . and the colors are, oh . . . like they're singing together! Just imagine, Grandpa . . . once Vincent was actually standing right next to these . . . shmeering them with his brush!

Grandpa just stood there, with both hands folded behind his back and a smile spreading across his face. And every time I glanced back at him, he was looking at *me* instead of the paintings!

When I finally told him I was ready to go, he brought me into the museum shop, where he showed me a large reproduction of Vincent's self-portrait.

"So . . . I thought you might like one of these." Grandpa smiled, handing me a long cardboard tube.

❖

When we got home that evening, my mom helped me unroll the poster, and we taped it to the wall above my bed.

I placed the cardboard tube in the back of my bedroom closet. Two years later, when we moved from 900 Bronx Park South to 3339 Wilson Avenue, I slipped the poster back into the tube, and hung it on my new bedroom wall.

When our family left the Bronx five years later, I carried the poster with me to the suburbs. And seven years after that, when I graduated from high school, I rolled the poster up once again and brought it with me to college.

Brothers
Neil Waldman
Oil on canvas

Chapter Six

Beneath the Bronx

⌁Though Brucie and I knew that all wasn't right between our parents, we had no idea that their nasty arguments would erupt into a full-blown war. Neither of us could have imagined that it would continue unrelenting through the early years of our childhood.

Late one night, during one of their loudest battles, I rose from bed and stood at the bedroom door as their voices ricocheted in from the living room.

I have to make it better. It's my job.

Reaching for the doorknob, I grasped it tightly. But no matter how hard I tried, I couldn't force my fingers to twist it open. Finally, my hand fell limply to my side as an ugly and discomforting idea was born in my mind.

I guess I must be a coward.

✌ ❖ ☞

As the morning sun rose over the tenements, its first rays pierced the screen of the bedroom window and struck my forehead. The blackness of my dream-world was suddenly red as I strained to open my eyes. Three blinks later, the silence was broken by my parents' angry voices. Their bedroom door opened and slammed shut, and my father's footfalls were loud in the hallway.

I tiptoed to the dresser and pulled out a sketch-pad. Sitting at my desk, I took out a bottle of India ink and began to draw. I sketched a mountain range speckled with lakes and forests. Atop the highest mountain, I concocted a castle with an iron gate, six cone-topped towers, and pennants billowing above the ramparts.

"What's that?" Brucie whispered from behind me.

You just get up?

"Yeah, The yelling woke me up. So . . . what's that you're drawing?"

Can't you see what it is? It's a castle.

"Yeah, but what castle is it?"

My castle!

"You mean, you have a castle?"

Yeah. I have a castle. Do you know what my real name is?

"Of course I know what your real name is! You're my big brother. Your name's Neil!"

That's not my real name.

"Well, what is your real name?"

King Neil.

Now, Brucie's eyes were nearly popping out of his head.

"You mean, you're a *king*?"

Yup.

"But you're only six years old! How can you be a king?"

I'm not really six years old.

"Well, where is your castle, anyway?"

In the Secret Kingdom.

"And just where is this Secret Kingdom?"

I looked past my little brother through the window to some white puffy clouds floating over the rooftops of the neighborhood.

It's under the Bronx.

"What?"

You heard me . . . it's under the Bronx.

"Really?"

Yup. Really!

"Well, what do you mean, it's under the Bronx?"

There are secret passageways all over the Bronx. Most of them are at the bottoms of sewers. Every sewer in the neighborhood. And if you climb all the way down, you'll find secret doors down there. And if you walk through one of those doors, guess what you'll see?

"That castle?" he said, pointing

Yup. That castle!

"Could you take me down there now?"

I've got bad news for you, Brucie. You see, there's a government down there. And governments have rules. And one of the rules in the Secret Kingdom is . . . nobody gets in till they're five.

Now Brucie screwed up his face, slapped his hand against his leg, and stormed out of the room. But he came back a few minutes later . . . and there was a smile on his face.

"I can wait," he said. "I'll be five after a while. So . . . could you tell me some more stories about that Secret Kingdom?"

Well, there's a white stallion down there. It's my stallion. And it's got a golden saddle and a golden sword. And . . . I'm married.

"You're married!"

Yup. I am. To a beautiful queen named Queen Marie. And every time I go down there, there's a servant waiting for me at the gate. And he puts a golden crown on my head, and he bows and says, "Welcome back, Your Majesty."

. . . And also, there's a pinto pony down there. All white with brown spots. And it's got a silver saddle and a silver sword. And it's waiting for you!

"Really?"

Yup. Really. And there's a princess down there, too. Princess Rossalie. And she's waiting to marry you.

"Me?" Brucie said, with his mouth dropping open.

Yup. You. You're gonna be called Prince Bruce!

⤞ ❖ ⤝

In the weeks that followed, I told Brucie story after story: stories of dragon slayers; stories of knights in shining armor; stories of military campaigns. But as the days followed one another, like a succession of falling leaves, I was getting more and more nervous about his upcoming birthday . . . And on the night before that dreaded day, I lay in my bed in the darkness, and heard a whisper from across the room.

"I can't sleep!"

What do you mean, you can't sleep?

"I'm too excited to sleep! When I get up in the morning, we're going down there! And I'm gonna get my pinto pony! And I'm gonna marry the princess!"

I took a deep breath.

I've got bad news for you, Brucie. The government just changed one of the rules. You have to be six to get in.

Brucie bolted up in bed. He stared at me and muttered, "If you weren't my big brother, your face would be covered in blood!"

He stormed out of the room and slammed the door. But a few minutes later, he returned, nodding his head.

"I can wait," he said, raising his eyebrows. "I'll be six after a while. So . . . could you tell me some more stories about the Secret Kingdom?"

Mommy
Neil Waldman
Colored pencil and watercolor

Chapter Seven

Our Mother's Wisdom

⌇Every night before bed, I'd tell Brucie stories about the Secret Kingdom . . . and after each story, he'd ask me how many days were left until his birthday. Then one afternoon, I got an idea. I spread a few pieces of oak tag out across the living-room floor, and the two of us started illustrating the stories. After a while, our mom started taping the illustrations to the kitchen walls, and before long, the walls were covered with them.

"I think the kitchen has become my favorite room in the apartment," she said. "Every time I walk in here, I feel like I'm entering a magical land."

"You are!" Brucie exclaimed. "It's called the Secret Kingdom!"

"Could you tell me about it?" she asked, but before Brucie could answer, I interrupted.

No! He can't. It really is secret!

"All right," she said. "Well, anyway, there's something else I wanted to share with you. You know how lucky we are to be living in this wonderful country."

The Windblown Hill
Neil Waldman
Oil on linen

"Sure," Brucie answered. "Grandma and Grandpa tell us about it all the time."

"Did you know that there are millions of people who live in places where things aren't so wonderful?"

You mean like the Old Country?

"Yes, That's right, Neilly, and in many other places as well. I was reading in the newspaper that in China people don't have enough to eat. In some villages over there, people are hungry almost all the time. Mothers make a soup out of dirt and boiling water to feed their families . . . because they have no meat, no potatoes, nothing.

"After a while, the dirt hardens in their stomachs. Most of them get very sick, and some even die. They know it will happen, but they drink the soup anyway . . . because they're so terribly hungry.

"So I have an idea," she continued.

She brought out a red and black coffee can, with a slot cut into its top.

"I thought that when any of us had an extra penny or two, we could drop them into this can. When it's full, we'll send it off to China."

"I've got a penny right now!" Brucie exclaimed, reaching into his pocket.

She handed him the coffee can, and Brucie dropped the coin into it. Then we decided to place the can on the shelf beside the Frigidaire . . . and before long, we turned the whole thing into a ritual. Every evening after dinner, Brucie and I would walk up to the shelf, reach into our pockets, and drop our spare change into the coffee can. After several months, we sent it off to China. A year later, we were filling a second can with the word *India* inscribed on it, and a year after that, we sent another one off to Ethiopia.

❦❖❧

It was also during those years that I came to realize that being Jewish meant that our family didn't celebrate Christmas or Easter, as our Irish and Italian neighbors did. But my understanding of what really made us different came on an autumn afternoon when Brucie was dealt a painful blow at the hands of one of his playmate's mothers.

I was sitting in front of the TV, wearing my cowboy shirt, ten-gallon hat, six-shooter, and silver-studded holster. Johnny Mack Brown, my favorite cowboy, smiled out at me from the TV screen when Brucie entered the room, sat down on the couch, and started sniffling.

You OK?

Brucie shook his head.

What happened?

"Billy's mother just told me that . . . that . . . after I die . . . my body's gonna get burnt up."

How's that?

"She says," he added, sobbing, "that Jews can't get into heaven. After I die I'm gonna end up . . . burning in hell . . . forever."

❦❖❧

"That's simply not true." Our mother's voice sounded as she strode into the room. Sitting down between us, she scooped Brucie up in her arms.

"Bru," she said, gently wiping Brucie's cheeks, "I have a story to tell you." I snuggled up next to her, and she began speaking.

"Long, long ago in the land of Israel, there was a kind rabbi who tried to help the people who had less than he had."

"Just like us."

"That's right, Bru. Just like us. Anyhow, this rabbi spent his life helping the sick, comforting the homeless, and feeding the hungry; and many people began to love him. Some people even believed that he had been sent to Earth by God."

You mean . . . they thought he was the Messiah?

"Yes, Neilly, that's exactly right. The rabbi kept helping people, and he became more and more popular. After a while, the Roman rulers got nervous because the rabbi was becoming more popular than they were. They were afraid that the people might rise up against them, so they decided to have him killed."

"Really?"

"Yes, really. Here's what they did to him. They hammered metal spikes through his wrists and ankles, nailing that poor man onto a wooden cross. Then they stood it up on the top of a hill in Jerusalem, where the rabbi slowly bled to death."

"After he died, some people began to believe that he was the Messiah, while some others felt that he was just a good and wonderful human being. The first group became Christians, while the others remained Jewish."

Is that why Jews and Christians have been having such a hard time getting along with each other all these years?

"Yes, that's exactly right, Neilly. You see, sometimes people feel threatened when someone doesn't agree with them."

"So, anyway, am I going to hell?" Brucie demanded.

"No. Of course not, Bru," she reassured him, tenderly kissing his forehead.

"And if you want to know the truth, I don't believe that such a place ever existed, anyway. I think that long, long ago, some leaders probably made the whole thing up in order to scare people into following them."

The Judgment
Bruce Waldman
Monoprint

Chapter Eight

School Woes

That summer, our sister, Bryna, was born, and three years later, little David came into the world. We moved from our apartment at 900 Bronx Park South to a row house with three bedrooms on Wilson Avenue in the Northeast Bronx.

On a sweltering September morning, my mother and I crossed Boston Road and walked along the sidewalks of Fish Avenue toward Public School 78. As perspiration beads oozed from my forehead and neck, streaming beneath my collar and soaking my already sticky undergarments, I looked up at the imposing brick school building through waves of heat that rippled up from the asphalt. We were ushered across Fish Avenue by a crossing guard, along with a converging mass of reassuring mothers and terrified first-graders, heading for their first day of school. Passing through the red school doors, we walked along an endless corridor and trudged up six metal staircases. We finally found Miss Bogel's room, a big square room with a wall of sun-baked windows and rows of wooden desks with glass inkwells and sculpted iron legs.

"Good morning," Miss Bogel greeted us with a raised eyebrow. "And who might this be?"

"Neil Waldman," was my mother's answer.

"Good morning, young man," Miss Bogel pronounced. "Welcome to first grade. Your seat is five-G, at the end of row five."

My mother walked me to the back of the room, placed my Johnny Mack Brown lunch box on the desk, and slipped an oatmeal cookie into my pocket. Then she slid a tin of colored pencils into the narrow space beneath the desktop, along with a box of pastels and two sketchpads. Finally, she wiped my forehead with her handkerchief and kissed me good-bye.

"We are going to have a very productive year, children," Miss Bogel announced as soon as my mother had left the room. "A lot will be required of you, and I expect that nearly all of you will be very good readers by June. If not, you'll be required to repeat first grade.

"You'll have to learn to write all twenty-six letters of the alphabet in both upper and lowercase, and to add and subtract all the numbers up to twenty. Now, are there any questions?"

I raised my hand.

"Yes," Miss Bogel pointed. "Five-G. What is it?"

Will we be doing any artwork?

"You are a first-grader now," Miss Bogel informed me sternly. "You will soon see that there'll be no time for kindergarten things in this classroom. I am sure that you will be extremely busy mastering the rudiments of English and mathematics."

❖

I never knew that I was myopic.

I'd always assumed that things just looked clearer up close. From behind my desk at the back of row five, it was difficult for me to see the groups of letters that Miss Bogel continuously scrawled across the blackboard.

I soon discovered that if I curled my index finger up against my thumb, pressed my hand in front of my eye, and peered through the narrow slit, I could usually decipher most of the blurry words.

But even with my new discovery, school wasn't going very well. I was far behind most of the others, and I spent hours drawing cartoon characters on the corners of my textbook pages that seemed to run and dance as I flipped through them. Although these "flip-books" were quite popular with my classmates, I wasn't learning to read.

Then, one Monday morning, as I lay in bed before the sun rose, I came up with a plan. After my mother woke me, I went straight to the bathroom as my father ate his breakfast and left the house. Then I tip-toed back into the bedroom. When I saw his car pulling out of the alleyway, I went downstairs, and approached my mother.

Mommy, my throat's killing me. I think I've got laryngitis.

"Sing me a song," she demanded, and I began croaking.

Day . . . vee . . . Day . . . vee . . . Crockett, King of the wild frontier.

"All right. You can stay home."

⌣∴❖∴⌢

On Tuesday morning, I used the same technique, and she fell for it again, so I tried it again on the following Monday.

By late November, I'd missed twelve days of school!

With Chanukah approaching, I decided to attempt something new. I told my mother that we got all eight days off.

"Really?" she said.

Yeah. Miss Bogel says that the Jewish kids don't have to go to school on Chanukah. It's like Christmas for the Catholics.

"All right," she said. "You can stay home."

I knew that this operation would be tricky because if my father ever found out what I was doing, I'd be in serious trouble. And so I spent every morning getting dressed, brushing my teeth, and pretending that I was preparing to leave for school while my father got ready to go to work. When he got into his car, I breathed a sigh of relief, took out my dreidel, and started playing with Brucie.

After missing six straight days of school, I decided that Chanukah was the greatest holiday of all!

❖

On a Thursday afternoon in March, Brucie and I were playing with our tin soldiers on the front stoop when I noticed a woman turning the corner onto Wilson Avenue. In a split second, I realized it was Miss Bogel! I bolted into the house, charged up the stairs into my bedroom, and dove under the blankets. A moment later, the doorbell rang.

I lay there frozen, with both hands pressed against my ears and the pillow covering my head. I didn't budge for what seemed like hours. Then my mother called me down to dinner. To my surprise, she never uttered a word about Miss Bogel's visit.

❖

As soon as my father left the house the next morning I was croaking again, but for the first time, it didn't work. After five pain-filled verses of "Davy Crockett," my mother stood there, defiantly pointing to the door. So I tried something new.

Please, Mommy, I don' wanna go to school. It's terribly horrible over there.

Now tears were streaming down my cheeks.

Please, Mommy. Please. Don' make me go!

She stepped toward the door and pushed it open. "Off you go," she demanded.

I crossed over the threshold, lumbered out onto the sidewalk, and looked back.

She pointed down the block.

I took one step and looked back at her with tear-filled eyes, but still she didn't budge.

So I took another step.

Fifteen minutes later, when I finally reached the distant corner, I looked back at her for the last time, and turned onto Boston Road.

That afternoon, Miss Bogel sent me down to the nurse's office, where I sat squinting before an eye chart. Two weeks later, I was wearing my first pair of glasses.

Chapter Nine

The Power of Journals

᠃**N**ow that I could see the blackboard, I began teaching myself to read. Within two or three months, I began catching up with the other kids, and with great excitement, I began adding subtitles to all the cartoons in my textbooks.

Then one morning, Miss Bogel stood before us, handed a speckled black-and-white composition book to every kid in class, and explained our first homework assignment.

"These are to be your journals," she began. "From now on, you'll each be expected to write at least one sentence every week about something you've experienced personally. It might be about an ice-cream cone that tasted delicious, or a birthday party that made you happy, or something that confused you or made you

Abe and Jessie
Bruce Waldman
Etching

feel bad. It doesn't matter what it was, as long as it really happened."

That night at dinner, my parents got into one of their terrible arguments. I don't even remember what it was about, but it was nasty. As the barbs flew back and forth across the dining room table, I quietly turned away and escaped to my bedroom. Closing the door behind me, I took out my new journal and wrote three words.

I am sad.

I stopped for a moment, and then I wrote again.

Mommy and Daddy make me sad.

Then I tried to describe everything I was feeling

inside: the knots in the pit of my stomach, the aching in my head, the tears forming in the corners of my eyes. When I finished writing, I began to read what I'd written, and almost like magic, the pain began to subside.

Misty Landscape
Neil Waldman
Oil on linen

By the time I was finished reading, the pain had disappeared completely! I was amazed. It seemed that I'd discovered a secret pathway that led from darkness to a land of sunshine.

A week later, I was angry at Brucie. Again, I turned to my journal and began writing.

I am mad.

Once again, I tried to describe everything I was feeling inside. I read what I'd written . . . and it worked again! So I kept on writing. Whenever I was having a bad day, I'd write about it in my journal . . . and nearly every time it helped me to get through the pain.

But there were many personal things I was feeling deep down inside. Things I didn't want anyone to know about. So I saved my allowance for three weeks and bought a second journal, a "secret" journal that I hid under my socks in one of my dresser drawers. I never showed it to Miss Bogel, my parents, or anyone else

❖

Over the years, writing would become a habit. Sometimes I'd write almost every day. At other times I'd go for weeks, or even months, without writing at all. But by the time I graduated from high school, there was a carton full of journals in the back of my bedroom closet.

Chapter Ten

Shabbos

᠊᠊Although our family rarely attended synagogue, my parents believed that Judaism was a rich cultural heritage that must be passed from generation to generation. We always celebrated the holidays at home, and the Sabbath, *Shabbos* as it's called in Yiddish, was an important and beautiful holiday that marked the end of every week.

Shabbos started just after the sun began to set on Friday evenings.

Bryna and I would spread our fanciest white tablecloth, and we'd set the table with embroidered napkins from the Old Country. Brucie would put out the dinner plates and silverware. Little David would just sit there, goo-gahing as he bounced up and down in his highchair.

The hustle-bustle of the school week seemed to fade in the soft evening light as the moon rose and the stars started twinkling in the sky. Mommy finished setting the table with our special *Shabbos* wine glasses. Then she'd cover the challah and pour the wine. A few minutes later, Brucie and I would fly down the stairs in shiny shoes, white shirts, and bow ties; and Bryna would dance into the dining room wearing a rhinestone tiara and a pink ballerina dress. We'd sit smiling across the *Shabbos* table as rich aromas beckoned from steamy soup bowls. Our mom would cover her head with her special *Shabbos* shawl, and light the candles. Then our father would lift the Kiddush cup, and begin his soulful chant.

"*Baruch ata Adonai* . . .

Blessed are you, O Lord our God, Creator of the universe, who has given us the fruits of the vine."

Now, it was my turn.

I'd rise up and close my eyes, resting both hands on the challah cover, thanking *Adonai* for bread.

Baruch ata Adonai . . .

Blessed are you, O Lord our God, Creator of the universe, who has brought forth bread from the earth.

Ripping six chunks from the fresh and fragrant challah, I'd pass one to each family member, and we'd begin to eat.

❖

Many years later, I came to realize how important the holidays and rituals of Jewish life had been to me.

I loved the stories, and the ethical questions within them touched me deeply. Because of them, I began asking myself questions about the differences between fair and unfair, good and evil, right and wrong. And the answers to those questions formed the roots that my life's tree would grow from.

Grandfather
Jean Morris
Etching

I soon began devouring books about Jewish history, Jewish culture, and the land of Israel. When I graduated from college, I went to live there, as an olive farmer on a kibbutz along the Jordan River, and visited many of the places I'd learned about during the holidays and rituals of my childhood. And it was several years after my return to New York that I began writing and illustrating Jewish books for children.

The Glutton
Jean Morris
Oil on canvas

Chapter Eleven

For the Love of Vincent

At P.S. 78, the students weren't allowed to use the library until second grade. And so Mrs. Golub, my second grade teacher, spent a long time preparing class 2-H for our first visit. She drew a big map of the library on the blackboard, explained how to use the card catalogue, and passed out a library card to every kid in class. Then Mrs. Golub told us that almost all the books in the library were there for us to borrow! In fact, we could take two books home every week, as long as we returned them on time.

I thrust my hand into the air.

"What is it, Neil?" she asked.

May we take two books out today?

"Yes, you certainly may."

Thank you!

"Now listen carefully, children," she continued, suddenly lowering her voice. "You must always remember to treat the library's books with the utmost care so that the students of P.S. 78 can continue using them for years to come."

She gave us the signal to stand, and we walked into the hallway in two straight lines: girls on the right, boys on the left. Arriving at the library door, we stopped, and Mrs. Golub raised a finger to her lips.

"Once we're inside," she whispered, "everyone must be quiet. Remember, people have come here to read."

⌁ ❖ ⌁

I walked through the doorway and scanned the room. Every wall was filled with books! Thick books, thin books, books with gold-edged pages, books with brown leather covers. More books than I'd ever seen in one place before.

I passed wide-eyed from shelf to shelf.

Arriving at last in the biography section, I began reading the titles of book after book, all neatly placed in alphabetical order. I walked from *A* to *B* to *C*, turned a corner, and high on the *V* shelf, I spotted the thin blue spine of a book and read the three silver words printed on it.

Vincent van Gogh

I quickly pulled the book from the shelf and

dropped to the floor. I flipped past the title page and the table of contents, anxious to discover why my mother would never tell me anything about Vincent's life. Then, as I began reading the book's first chapter, I learned why.

"The wildly intense colors and slashing brush-strokes of Vincent van Gogh's paintings are clues that speak to us of his short and emotion-filled life. He suffered terribly through his days in poverty, misunderstood, and without any friends except his brother Theo.

"Though this disturbed genius once cut his own ear off in a fit of drunken stupor, and ended his own life with a pistol shot to the chest at the age of thirty-seven, most tragic is the fact that he lived his life misunderstood by others and utterly alone in the world. The works of this great master were not appreciated until after his death."

As I sat there on the library floor, reading about my hero, my eyes welled up with tears. I closed the book and began to cry.

What happened next was my seven-year-old way of dealing with pain far greater than anything I could handle. I began to fantasize.

Suddenly, I was flying. I crossed the Atlantic and arrived in southern France, where I came upon a red-bearded artist standing before his easel in an olive grove.

Would it be okay if I watched?

"Yes," he answered, "but please don't speak to me while I'm painting."

I sat on the grass and looked on in amazement as he dabbed his canvas again and again with his brush. Then he put his brush down and sat right next to me. I stared at his painting and gasped. The colors seemed to be glowing, swirling, sparkling!

You must be very famous. I think I once saw one of your paintings in a museum.

The man chuckled.

"That's very kind of you," he said, "but you're mistaken. You see, except for my brother, no one has ever understood my work. I once put some paintings in a gallery, and people said that they were garbage. Someone even wrote that my paintings were the work of a wild animal."

Well, I think they're crazy! This is one of the most beautiful paintings I've ever seen! I'm sure that if people in New York could see your paintings, they'd know how amazing they are, too!

"New York?" he mused. "Is that where you're from?"

Uh-huh.

"I've always wanted to go there," he said sadly, "but it's such a long voyage. And besides, I don't have any money."

Well, I can take you there for free!

"You're joking!" he exclaimed.

No, I'm not. Come follow me, and I'll show you how.

He began folding his easel, and he handed me a roll of canvas and a box of oil paints.

❖

More than forty years later, I was having lunch with Larry Rosler, my editor at Boyds Mills Press. We were talking about childhood fantasies, and when I told him about meeting Vincent in the south of France, we decided that I should turn it into a book. When the book was completed, we called it *The Starry Night*.

The Fur Coat
Jean Morris
Etching

Chapter Twelve

Cancer

᭘ That August, an official-looking letter arrived from school stating that I'd be in Mrs. Brown's class. I was relieved. All the kids knew that Mrs. Brown was the coolest teacher in third grade. Aside from being a terrific teacher, she was a kind and caring person. But, although I had no way of knowing it, I was about to walk into trying times.

It all started one evening at dinner.

Brucie and Bryna were joking with each other when our father suddenly slammed his fist on the table, stood up, and started yelling at them.

"Until you kids learn to behave yourselves like normal human beings," he growled, "I'm going to eat in peace and quiet!"

With that, he stormed out of the dining room . . .

and it would be more than a year before he sat at the table with us again.

He'd stay by himself in the living room, reading his newspapers and watching the evening news while we gulped down our supper. We'd always speak in measured whispers, doing everything we could not to disturb him. After we finished, Mommy would clear the table, rinse the dishes, and set one place for him. Then, after she led the four of us up the stairway to our bedrooms, he'd click off the TV and lumber into the dining room.

During those tension-filled days, I began to miss Grandpa Meyer terribly. He hadn't visited us in weeks, and our father had stopped driving us to Daly Avenue for the Saturday visits that had once been an expected and looked-forward-to part of our lives.

"Grandpa hasn't been feeling very well lately," Mommy explained when I asked her about him, "and your father is very worried."

So I went upstairs and lay down on my bed. Looking up at the poster of Vincent, I remembered the day when Grandpa bought it for me. I walked over to my desk, took out my colored pencils, and started sketching the two of us looking out across New York Harbor at the Statue of Liberty. Underneath the drawing I wrote him a note:

> *Dear Grandpa,*
> *I hope you get better soon. Then maybe we could go to the zoo or something. I miss you.*
> *Love, Neilly*

It was several weeks later that my mom told me that Grandpa was in the hospital.

"He's very sick," she explained, "and he might have to be in the hospital for a while."

Could we go see him?

"I'm sorry, Neilly," she answered, "but children aren't allowed in that part of the hospital."

I walked into my bedroom and closed the door. Looking up at the poster of Vincent, I started thinking about the things Grandpa and I had done together. I thought of the days at the zoo when we sat there watching the Mother Herd. I remembered looking down at the seals from my perch on Grandpa's shoulders. And then I thought of the first time he took me to the Loew's Paradise, that amazing movie theatre on the Grand Concourse.

Grandpa had told me that the Paradise was *a truly unbullivable picture house,* and as usual, he was right. When we passed through the big glass doors and stepped onto the soft red carpets, I spun around . . . and my eyes almost popped out of my head! All the walls were decked with huge oil paintings in carved golden frames . . . paintings of snow-capped mountains and golden sunsets and tropical islands. Up above them hung sparkling chandeliers and sculptures of amazing creatures that Grandpa called *gar-goyuls.*

After buying me a pack of chocolate bonbons, Grandpa led me through the lobby and into the theatre. We snuggled into velvety seats, and Grandpa pointed toward the ceiling.

"Have a looky up there," he said.

I leaned back and stared at the most amazing ceiling I'd ever set eyes on. It looked just like the night sky, all painted dark blue, with thousands of twinkling light bulbs that looked just about like real stars. And underneath the ceiling, puffy clouds floated by!

Are those clouds really real?

"Could be," Grandpa said, "but they might be made out of smoke or steam or something."

Just then the stars started dimming, and the audience hushed. As organ music filled the theatre and titles began rolling across the humongous screen, Grandpa leaned over and whispered in my ear. "It's a 'Stan and Ollie' picture," he said. "The funniest guys alive!"

I could see right away that Grandpa was right again. Skinny little Stan started doing really dumb things, like stuffing a banana peel into his back pocket or hiding a lit cigar under a rug. After a while, big fat Ollie would be sniffing for smoke, and then he'd go bonkers and start screaming at Stan, hitting him with his hat and chasing him around the room. And while that was going on, Grandpa pressed his hand over his mouth, slapped his knees, and started belly laughing. After a while, I was watching Grandpa instead of the screen. By the time the movie ended, my sides were killing me.

❖

I didn't get to see Grandpa for over a month. Then, on a Saturday morning, our father walked into the bedroom.

"We're going to the hospital," he told Brucie and me, and within minutes, we all slid into the Nash Rambler. As we zoomed past the stores on Boston Road, our mom turned and started speaking.

"Grandpa's going to be outside for the first time today," she said, "and lots of people are coming to see him. He's quite weak, and he might not be able to talk with you. You should know that he's lost a lot of weight. He may look different from the way you remember him."

After parking the car, we walked out onto the sidewalk in front of a big gray building. Grandma Gussie was standing there with Tanta Annie, Uncle Hick and Aunt Thelma, Uncle Cal and Aunt Jeanie, Uncle Louie and Tanta Esther, along with three bearded men in black suits whom I'd never seen before.

Our father left us, and after a while he walked out of the hospital pushing a wheelchair. Slumped on the wheelchair, wearing a blue bathrobe, with blankets wrapped around his legs, was Grandpa Meyer. He had an empty look on his face, and he didn't seem to notice any of us as he passed me by. Within seconds, all the grownups gathered around him. Mommy stood with us on the outer edge of the crowd. I kept craning my neck, trying to see between the bodies, hoping for a glimpse of my Grandpa. Then, after a long while, the relatives parted, and Mommy walked us up to the wheelchair. Grandpa looked at me, smiled weakly, and touched my hand. Then we walked back to the car.

❖

I only got to see Grandpa one more time.

He was sitting on the living-room couch in the apartment on Daly Avenue, surrounded by a sobbing sea of tantas, cousins, uncles, and friends from the Old Country. I looked at Grandpa's shriveled face, but his eyes didn't seem to be able to see me. They stared past me from eye sockets that looked like dark caves.

I love you, Grandpa.

I kept on whispering to him, hoping that some-how he might be able to hear me, but I never found out if he did.

In school that week, Mrs. Brown asked if anyone in class knew what cancer was.

I raised my hand.

I do. My Grandpa's got it.

Chapter Thirteen

Reckoning

On the night before Brucie's sixth birthday, I looked out across the darkening bedroom and informed my little brother that the government of the Secret Kingdom had prevented his entry yet again.

They changed the rules. You have to be seven to get in.

As in the previous year, Brucie grimaced and bolted from the room, only to return a minute later with a smile on his face.

"I can wait," he said, nodding. "Do you think you could tell me another story about the Secret Kingdom?"

❖

I was in fourth grade then. Brucie was in second, and my mother had given me my first real job: walking my little brother to and from school every day.

While meandering toward Wilson Avenue on a sun-drenched afternoon, Brucie and I discovered a triangular lot between three intersecting streets. There weren't any houses on it. Neither were there any stores or apartment buildings — just grass, overgrown weeds, and a hand-painted sign that read:

LAND FOR SALE

ROSEN REAL ESTATE

OLinville 3-0217

We crossed the street and began to explore.

Entering a world sprinkled with bottle caps, shredded newspapers, and small yellow flowers, we crunched through the waist-high grasses. I grabbed both of Brucie's hands, and we started spinning gleefully. Round and round we spun, growing dizzier and dizzier, until we lost our balance. Floating in slow motion through the air, we landed softly in a clump of weeds and sat there smiling as the world kept swirling around us.

Grandpa Meyer used to take me to a place like this in the zoo. Look up, Brucie. Isn't it amazing!

"Oh yeah!" Brucie exclaimed. "Sure is. I can't even see a single building. Feels like we're in the jungle!"

We dropped onto our backs and wiggled like worms until we were comfortable.

Hey, let's imagine that all the animals in the jungle are our palzers. We can ride around on lions' backs with all the other animals following right behind us.

"Just like the Thanksgivings Day Parade!"

Yeah . . . Let's close our eyes and pretend it's really happening.

"Okeedokie!"

Brucie rested his head on my shoulder, and I drifted off into jungle dreams.

Andean Landscape
Neil Waldman
Oil on linen

The weeds turned into giant redwoods. Mosquitos became pterodactyls. The mud puddle beyond our feet was magically transformed into a blue lagoon, where I swam with schools of iridescent fish. I imagined that all the animals were my friends. I hopped onto the back of a lion who started bounding through the jungle. Followed by herds of zebras, antelopes, and giraffes, I leapt off the lion's back, flew up into the treetops and started playing with a family of monkeys, swinging from tree to tree. Then I soared higher still, corkscrewing around the rainbow with a flock of golden birds.

Then suddenly, Brucie was shaking my shoulder.

"Hey, Neilly," he demanded, "is the Secret Kingdom really real or have you been making it up all along?"

I looked around, remembering where we were.

Nope. It's really there, way down under the ground.

"Well, I'm starting to think you've been lying to me."

No way!

"Then take me down there now. See that sewer over there. Let's go down!"

Don't you remember the rules?

"I'm starting to think that there aren't really any rules!"

As soon as you turn seven I'll take you down.

"I don't believe you! If there really is a Secret Kingdom, you'd better take me down right now. Otherwise I know you're a dirty rotten liar!"

Looking at my little brother shaking his head, I took a deep breath.

Yeah. You're right, Brucie. I have been lying to you all along. So, are you going to hate me for the rest of your life?

Brucie looked away and grumbled.

"I really wanted that pony!"
But a moment later he turned back toward me.
"How could I ever hate you? You're my big brother. I love you more than anything on earth!"

I'm really sorry.

"Yeah, that's OK," Brucie answered. "Now, could you tell me another story about the Secret Kingdom?"

Fields
Jean Morris
Etching

Daddy
Bruce Waldman
Pen and ink

Chapter Fourteen

Queen Marie

~: **W**hen Brucie and I returned home from the green triangle, the Nash Rambler was parked there in front of the house. We carefully opened the door and tiptoed upstairs toward our bedroom. But when we neared the top step, he was right there, looming over us like the Creature from the Black Lagoon.

"What are you two doing home so late? School was over hours ago!"

I lowered my head and waited for the coming storm.

"Next time I'll report you to the t r u a n t o f f i - c e r ! " he thundered in a voice that grew louder with each word. "He'll know what to do w i t h y o u ! ! ! "

Brucie and I stood as still as statues, and after a while, our father raged past us and rumbled down the stairs.

Rhinoceros
Bruce Waldman
Monoprint

❖

Past midnight, I was awakened by my parents' angry voices. I sat up in bed, opened the bedroom door, and walked to the top of the stairs.

I have to help them. It's my fault Daddy's always mad.

I wiped my forehead with my pajama sleeve and returned to the bedroom. Sitting at my desk, I took out my colored pencils and sketchpad, and started drawing. I sketched a castle on a hill, surrounded by a moat overflowing with snakes and crocodiles.

From the far corner of the room, Brucie sat up in bed.

"They yelling again?"

Yeah.

"I hate it."

Me, too.

Brucie got out of bed, and walked over to me.
"You sure can draw! It's the Secret Kingdom, isn't it?"

Yup.

"Those snakes are totally cool!"

Then, after a while, Brucie yawned and returned
to bed. But I kept drawing late into the night. The sun's
rays awakened me, slumped over with my face pressed
against my sketchpad.

❖

In school that day, I got the opportunity to do
some more artwork. It was Friday, and Mr. Broadwell
arrived in our classroom pushing a cartful of art supplies. The tall bald-headed art teacher stood before the
class and explained our assignment in a voice that
sounded like music.

"Today, people, you may paint whatever you wish."
That was all I had to hear.

I fetched a tin and a set of watercolors, and
returned to my desk. In pencil, I sketched a stallion
ridden by a king wielding a long curved sword. In the
background, I painted a land of jungles, exploding

volcanos, and rivers of lava, with a castle standing on the edge of a humongous cliff. I was sketching the stormy skies above the castle when Mr. Broadwell's voice invaded my kingdom.

"Class is nearly over," he sang out. "Now it's time for each of you to show us what you've done."

One by one, my classmates stood and displayed their artwork. When I held up my watercolor, Mr. Broadwell stopped me.

"That's quite intriguing, Neil," he chirped, nodding. "Could you tell us something about it?"

It's a picture of a king of a secret kingdom deep down in the center of the earth.

"Intriguing concept. Good show, young man!"

After class, a bunch of kids crowded around my desk. Richie Greenberg asked me to tell him more about the Secret Kingdom. Monty Weiner asked about my watercolor technique. Marie Portobella, the prettiest girl in class, remained long after the others had left.

"I wish I could paint amazing pictures like you," she said.

You could. It just takes practice.

"But I wouldn't even know where to start." Marie shrugged.

I mustered up all my courage.

I could show you how.

"Really?"

Sure. I could show you at recess next week.

"Yes," she said quietly, as if speaking to herself. "I'd love that."

I felt a shiver pass through me as I sat there with goose bumps spreading over my arms.

"See you on Monday." Queen Marie smiled as she turned and waltzed out of the room.

❖

At 10:45 on Monday morning, the recess bell sounded, and kids jumped up from their desks. Like sharks headed for a feeding frenzy, they shoved, squeezed, and funneled through the doorway, racing down the corridors and pouring out onto the schoolyard.

Once the classroom had emptied, I watched a beaming Queen Marie zigzagging toward me. Pulling out my box of colored pencils, I stood and offered Her Majesty my chair. Queen Marie slipped in behind my desk, and looked up at me with hope-filled eyes as I placed a royal-blue pencil in her hand.

I'd like to begin by teaching you everything about shading.

"Neatsy-keen," she bubbled. "I've been thinking about this all weekend!"

And so our tutorial began.

Over five perfect days, I instructed Her Majesty in the fine arts of smudging, smoothing, and shmeering. But on Friday afternoon, our lessons came to a chilling end on the unforgiving sidewalks of Fish Avenue.

It happened suddenly, unexpectedly, just after the dismissal bell rang. I was passing through the schoolyard gate when someone crashed into me, sending my books flying.

"Gee, I'm sorry." Rufus Blood laughed.

I bent down and began gathering my books.

He shoved me again, and this time I landed on the sidewalk.

"Oops," he said. "Sorry, four-eyes. I guess I must've slipped."

I looked around and saw that a crowd had gathered. I lunged at Blood, grabbing his waist, and we went hurtling through the air, thumping onto the pavement. He spun, and the next thing I knew, he was on top of me. He pressed my face into the concrete, yanked my arm behind me, and began twisting my wrist upward, forcing it toward the back of my neck.

Owww!!!

"Give?" Blood yelled.

No!

He pushed my wrist higher.

Owwwowwwowww!

"Give?"

No!

He forced it even higher . . . until the pain was unbearable.

"Give?"

Yeah, yeah, yeah. I give! I give!

Blood let go, jumped up, and was immediately engulfed by a mob of well-wishers.

"Way to go!" said Monty Weiner, slapping Blood on the back.

"You wiped his butt!" said Bobby Sampson.

I sat there alone, watching the horde drifting away down Fish Avenue. I recognized several neighbors, classmates, and supposed friends, laughing as they showered Blood with wide-eyed praises. Among them, I spotted Queen Marie.

❖

After the recess bell sounded on the following Monday, I waited hopefully at my desk, but Marie Portobella was swallowed by the masses, swarming out onto the schoolyard.

Sitting alone in the silent classroom, I lowered my face between folded arms, closed my eyes, and began slipping across the oceans of my imagination. I could taste the salty air, feel the sea breeze on my forehead, hear the footfalls of my leather boots on the *Dolphin's* wooden decks. Climbing to the masthead, I lifted myself into the crow's nest. Perched high above the billowing sails, I took out my spyglass and started scanning the southeasterly seas. My eyes widened and my breath suddenly froze, for there, upon the horizon, sat the New Seaflores, a chain of volcanic atolls revered for the finest coral, spices, and sapphires.

Back in the empty classroom, I opened my eyes, lifted my head off the desktop, and began to draw. I sketched the *Dolphin's* crow's nest, and within it I drew a brave sea captain peering out across the sea. On his head I crafted a three-pointed pirate's hat, complete with skull and crossbones. Hanging from his belt, I drew a jewel-studded sword.

And as the sharks thrashed back into the classroom, I rendered the sword's long crescent blade, and massaged its handle of polished whalebone with my pencil.

The Pink Trees
Neil Waldman
Oil on canvas

Chapter Fifteen

Woodstock

It took me a while to get over the loss of Queen Marie, but before long, she'd been dethroned in a bloodless coup, replaced by a kinder, more beautiful new queen. Her name was Queen Kathy, and her benevolent reign fostered days of peace and tranquility in the Secret Kingdom, like mirror reflections of the gentle quiet that had begun to settle over the troubled lands of the East Bronx.

Then, toward the end of June, Aunt Jeanie phoned, inviting me to spend a week with her family in the Catskill Mountains. Uncle Hick, the coolest uncle of all time, would be over next Sunday to pick me up, and I was psyched. Traveling with Uncle Hick would probably be outrageous.

Brucie and I had always known that Uncle Hick was really a kid in disguise. At family gatherings, he'd leave the grown-ups and spend hours playing with us. Wearing a big white cowboy hat and swinging a rope, he'd loosely tie all the cousins to the banister at the foot of the stairs and pretend not to notice as we escaped. Then he'd track us down one by one, rope us, and tie us to the banister again.

But that's not all.

It was Uncle Hick who bought me my first jigsaw puzzle: a big green and brown puzzle of Johnny Mack Brown, waving from a rearing stallion. It was Uncle Hick who built a set of swings for Brucie and me on the patch of dirt across the alleyway behind our house. And it was Uncle Hick who was about to drive me out of the city for the first time.

✦❖✦

Rip Van Winkle Lake
Maurice Meyer
Acrylic on Masonite

On Sunday morning, I rose before the sun and sat waiting on the front stoop with Brucie. I looked at the sparkling white sneakers that my mom had just bought for me.

"You've never been to the mountains," she explained, "and you'll need a sturdy pair of shoes to run around in. You'll be out in the woods for a week, and I'm sure you'll have a lot of exploring to do."

I jumped up when I saw Uncle Hick's laundry truck turning the corner onto Wilson Avenue. By the time he pulled up in front of our house, I was waiting beside the curb.

"Howdy, pardner!"

Uncle Hick doffed his hat as he stepped out onto the sidewalk. "I hear you're hankerin' for an adventure in the wilderness."

Yup! Sure am!

Uncle Hick took my cardboard suitcase from Mommy, lifted the rear hatch, and slid it in. I kissed everyone good-bye, and jumped onto the passenger seat. Within seconds, we were on our way.

As we drove northward through the Bronx, the tapestry of tightly knit apartment buildings gave way to a patchwork of private homes, sculpted bushes, and manicured lawns. Now the houses were fewer and farther apart, until we glided into a panorama of meadows speckled with wildflowers, sparkling streams, and rolling green hills.

"So whad'ya think of the wilderness, pardner?" Uncle Hick asked.

Bee-you-tee-ful!

"Ya know," he said, smiling, "I was born and raised in the Catskills, and every time I drive up into this neck of the woods, I get mighty happy."

"We moved to the Bronx from the village of Tannersville when I was a little squirt. Well, the city slickers started calling me 'Hick,' and I reckon I kinda liked it. So whad'ya think I did?"

You decided to keep the name?

"You're one perdy smart dude, pardner." Uncle Hick winked, mussing my hair with his big hand.

Crossing the Hudson River at a place called Bear Mountain, the views grew more and more breathtaking. With the winding blue river far below us on the right and the Catskills rising up on the left, we passed through the town of Kingston, and Uncle Hick began to sing:

"I'm an ole cowhand,
    from the Rio Grande.
I can rope a steer,
    any time of year."

Before long, we were crooning together. From "Yippie-tie-yie-yo" to "The Red River Valley" and "The Streets of Laredo," we sang every cowboy song I'd ever heard. Then, with the narrow country road meandering for miles beside a mountain stream, we turned to the right and rolled onto the main street of a country village.

"Well, this is it, pardner," Uncle Hick nodded. "Another minute and we'll be at Cal and Jeanie's place."

We rounded a bend, and there before us were

Grandma Gussie, Aunt Jeanie, and Uncle Cal sitting on folding chairs before a big old barn. Little cousin Jefferson was just behind them, playing with a set of red metal fire trucks. We turned onto a gravel driveway, and they all started walking toward us. I jumped out of the truck and bounded up to them.

"Welcome to Woodstock," Uncle Cal said, giving me a big hug.

❖

In the generations that preceded my own, there were already a number of artists in the family. Grandpa Meyer used to tell me about one of his tantas who loved to paint in watercolor, and Grandpa himself always kept a pile of sticks in his bedroom closet. He'd whittle them into walking sticks that looked like totem poles stacked with fantastic creatures. Maurice Meyer, my "Uncle Hick," was an artist, too. Hick began painting landscapes at the age of 70, nostalgic scenes rich with memories of his boyhood years in Tannersville.

But it was Jean Morris, my father's youngest sister, who had been deemed a prodigy from the early years of her childhood. Indeed, Aunt Jeanie had won a silver medal in a national art competition at the age of 12, and her oil painting of the tenements of our East Bronx neighborhood had traveled to museums and galleries throughout the country.

During the days I spent in Woodstock, I'd peek through the window at Jeanie as she stood before an

The Falls at Horseshoe Curve
Maurice Meyer
Acrylic on canvas

old wooden easel in the barn she turned into a studio that summer. I loved her palette streaked with swirls of rainbow color. I loved the stacks of canvases, waiting to be painted. I loved the bottles crammed with brushes of every size and shape. I loved the sweet-smelling rags soaking in linseed oil. I loved it all.

Someday, I promised myself, *I'm going to live in a beautiful green place and have a studio just like this one.*

After I arose on that first morning, I discovered that Uncle Hick had already left for the city.

"He didn't want to wake you up," Grandma Gussie explained. "He'll be back next weekend. Now, come into the kitchen. Eat some breakfast."

After a bowl of oatmeal and a glass of orange juice, I walked out past the barn and crossed the road. In the distance, I saw a boy approaching on a bicycle. Reaching me, he stopped and dismounted.

"You Neil?" he asked.

Yup.

"Well, I'm your second cousin Mortimer. You can call me Morty. Morty Schnepps."

Oh, yeah. My mom told me about you. You live around here, right?

"I live in town. Want me to show you around?"

Sure thing.

"Hop on," Morty said, tapping his bike. I settled onto

the bar between the saddle and handlebars. Then Morty shoved off and we were on our way. Speeding down a series of winding hills, we turned onto a trail in the woods.

"From here on," Morty said, "we go on foot."

So where are we going?

"The Thousand Ponds."

What's that?

"One of the coolest places on the face of the earth." Morty leaned the bicycle against a tree, and we started hiking. The trail turned downward into grassy marshlands, where we jumped from stepping-stone to stepping-stone, doing our best to avoid slipping into the slimy marsh bottom. Then we crossed to the other side, climbed a hill, and reentered the cool shade of the forest.

"Ever seen a fire toad?" Morty asked.

Nope.

"What about a snapping turtle?"

Nope.

"Salamander?"

Nope. We don't have any of those in the Bronx.

"Well, what kind of critters do you have?"

Lions, Siberian tigers, grizzly bears . . .

"Really?"

Yup, really!

"You're not pulling my leg?"

Nope. I'm not.

"Well, if I could get over for a visit, do you think you could show them to me?"

Sure thing!

"Cool. OK," he said, suddenly slowing his pace. "We're getting close now. Do you hear them?"

What?

"Just keep walking," he whispered. "You'll hear them in a minute."

We climbed a hill, and as we began descending on the far side, I could just make out a quiet humming sound in the distance. Morty turned to me with his finger pressed against his lips.

As we continued, the humming grew steadily louder. Then, after a while, I could hear chirps, and soon the chirps were joined by croaks, bleeps, and whistles.

What are they?

"You'll see in a minute. Wait here till I call you."

Morty slipped silently between the trees. Entering a grove of leafy bushes, he stopped and slowly lowered himself to the ground. Then he beckoned with his hand. I made my way toward him as quietly as I could, but a dead branch snapped beneath my sneaker, and suddenly the forest hushed. I froze, and continued toward him on tiptoe. Arriving at Morty's side, I slowly dropped to my knees.

Before us was a large clearing. There were mosses and yellow flowers as far as I could see. There were several smooth white boulders strewn about like dinosaur eggs, and there was an endless array of ponds that reflected the cloud-sprinkled sky like mirrors.

We sat motionless for a long time, and slowly the humming started up again in the distance. Now it grew steadily louder, like an approaching airplane, until the air was vibrating with croaks, chirps, and whistles.

Morty lifted his hand and pointed to a small spotted frog sitting in the nearest pond. The pouch beneath its chin inflated like a balloon, and the frog emitted a sound like a long vibrating musical note, *rrrrrr-cht*. Then, from the mossy shore of the next pond, came the reply, *rrrrrr-cht*.

In another pond, I spotted a dark-brown frog with all four legs stretched out just below the water's surface. Then I spotted another, and another. As I scanned the ponds, I counted more than ten.

"Pretty cool, huh?" Morty whispered.

Totally cool!

"We'll come back tomorrow with sandwiches and coffee cans, and spend all day, and catch as many as we can. But not now. They'll be waiting for us. We should get back for lunch."

Morty turned, and I took a last look at the ponds as we started walking back toward his bike.

꜀❖꜀

A wonderful week passed, and Uncle Hick didn't show up.

"He'll get back here as soon as he can," Uncle Cal assured me. "He called last night and said he's going to try to be here tomorrow. He says things are very busy at the laundry."

But Uncle Hick didn't come the next day, or the day after that, or the day after that. And so, Morty and I continued frolicking together. He lent me his sister's bike, and we spent our days riding over every inch of Woodstock. We'd usually meet at the general store, and after sharing a chocolate malt or a black-and-white ice cream soda, we'd go exploring. On sweltering afternoons, we'd go skinny-dipping at a place called "the log," where I met a couple of Morty's classmates. But we spent most of our time hiking through the woods.

We returned to the Thousand Ponds again and again, and caught all kinds of critters.

Then, while running through a grassy field one afternoon, we bumped right into a box turtle with an unusual marking on her shell that looked almost like the letter *J*. So we took her home and decided to call her Josephine.

Each afternoon, Morty and I returned from the Ponds, and our collection grew and grew. In six days, we'd caught twelve frogs, eleven toads, three painted turtles, and five salamanders.

"We have to make a home for all these critters," Morty said as he stared at the teeming shoe boxes and coffee cans on the ground beside the barn.

"You know, we could build a really cool zoo."

Great idea! Let's get started!

So we began digging a hole in the dirt behind the barn, set an old window screen on top of it, and called it "Toad Hall." Then we found a tin washbasin in an abandoned shed, put some rocks and water into it, and filled it with frogs, painted turtles, and salamanders. Lastly, we built a home for Josephine, stuffing a wooden apple crate with pebbles and grass.

And we had to feed them all: live insects for the painted turtles, frogs, and toads; fish food for the salamanders; and a saucer of chopped radishes, lettuce, and slices of tomato for Josephine.

Of all the critters, Josephine was the only one that wasn't afraid of us. After a couple of days, she was eating lettuce right out of our hands.

Then, on a sad Sunday, we found three of the salamanders floating belly-up in the washbasin. Morty fished them out, and we decided to give them a proper funeral, burying them in the woods behind the barn. Morty delivered a eulogy.

"We're really sorry, guys," he began. "I've never kept any animals in cages before, and I didn't think you'd die. I hope you'll forgive us someday. Have a good time in Heaven. Amen."

We each placed three stones on the grave site, and

as we began walking toward the bikes, an idea popped into my head.

Maybe we should return the others to the ponds.

"You know, I think you're right," Morty agreed.

So we scooped up the painted turtles and the two remaining salamanders, put them in a coffee can, and hiked back into the woods. Next morning, we returned with two coffee cans of frogs and a shoe box filled with toads.

Now only Josephine remained.

We carried her onto the grassy field across the road that evening, and said good-bye. As we started walking away, she stuck her head out of her shell. She kept looking at us as we headed back toward the barn.

But when I stepped outside the next morning, I found Josephine sitting right next to her crate beside the barn.

"I've never heard of anything like this!" Morty said when he arrived a minute later. "Maybe we should take her deeper into the woods."

So we went hiking for about an hour or so, and left Josephine in a grove of birch trees. But two days later, she found her way back to the wooden crate again.

This time, we decided to take her to a meadow on the other side of town.

"It's a really beautiful place," Morty said, "complete with a stream and a great view. I think she'll love it there."

We placed Josephine in a shoe box that I held under my right arm, and I gingerly climbed onto my bicycle as Morty held me steady. Then he hopped onto his bike, and we started peddling down the road. When we got back home, Uncle Hick's laundry truck was waiting on the driveway.

⋄

Before I knew it, I was back in the Bronx.

My mom never let me wear those brand-new sneakers again. Eleven days of romping through the Catskills had turned them brown and filled them full of holes.

Then, on a Saturday in late July, a postcard arrived with a photograph of some mountains and a beautiful sunset on it. Spread out across the sky, in bright yellow script, were four words: *HELLO from the CATSKILLS!* I flipped the postcard over and started reading the note on the other side.

> *Dear Neil,*
>
> *You're not going to believe this! Yesterday when I got home from the ponds, Josephine was just sitting there, right next to the back door! And guess what? My mom says I can keep her! If you could get up to Woodstock before summer ends, she will still be here.*
>
> > *Your second cousin,*
> > *Morty*
>
> *PS: Josephine told me to tell you that she really misses you.*

Chapter Sixteen

Lewisohn Stadium

As the last days of summer slid slowly toward September, Brucie, Bryna, David, and I spent our time sitting together on the living-room floor with paints and colored pencils.

It seemed to me that we drifted through the daylight hours in a world of friendly sunshine. Our mother was a gentle creature who gathered us around her like a great hen. She'd spread her protective wings across the far corners of the neighborhood, spinning tales about the wonders of the earth, feeding us graham crackers and strawberries, and warning us of the dangers that lay hidden in the shadowy world outside.

We knew that in all the universe, there was only one creature more powerful than she, and that creature was our father. He'd return from work after the sun disappeared, and all feelings of security would evaporate. As he entered the house, the stairs would tremble beneath his footsteps, sending tremors through the walls. He always arrived in darkness, like an approaching storm. And when he spoke, bolts of lightning exploded within and without, leaving my heart pounding with fear.

～∴❖∴～

Brucie and I were playing in the alleyway one evening, when our father emerged from the back door.

"Neil," he called out, "get washed and get into the car."

I looked back at Brucie as I followed my father into the house. Slipping up the stairs to the bathroom, I scrubbed my hands, arms, neck, and face. A minute later, I slid onto the back seat of the Nash Rambler. Now my father was coming toward me. Yanking the door open, he pulled himself in behind the steering wheel.

"You sit up front with me, Nooly," he said.

I was perplexed.

He almost never called me that. And I'd never been allowed in the front seat before. Still, I did exactly as I was told.

As we pulled out of the alleyway and turned onto Wilson Avenue, my confusion grew. I'd never been alone with my father before.

Fearful thoughts began pulsing through my brain.

My mom had shown me a series of old newspaper articles about the Lindbergh kidnapping, from the first shocking headlines to the last gruesome photos of the baby's body.

Maybe he's gonna kidnap me. I'll never see Mommy, Brucie, or the babies again.

My father drove beyond the streets of the neighborhood. We crossed over a muddy river on a gray metal drawbridge, and I was convinced that something terrible was about to happen. I gritted my teeth, mustered all my courage, and asked the dreaded question.

. . . Daddy . . . where . . . are . . . we . . . going?

"To Lewisohn Stadium."

I had no idea of what Lewisohn Stadium was, but I was too afraid to ask a second question, so I just sat there.

My father parked the car on a shady side street, took hold of my hand, and led me down a dark alleyway. We turned a corner, and came upon a line of grown-ups standing before a concrete wall. Standing at the end of the line, we began shuffling toward a man in a dark blue uniform.

"Here, Nooly, give these to him," my father said, placing two tickets in my hand.

We passed through the gate and stepped into a colossal amphitheater. I looked around, and my mouth dropped open.

Right there in front of us was a great stage filled with men in black suits and women in long white dresses.

Some were standing. Others were seated. And they were all tooting woodwinds, banging tympani, blowing trumpets, plucking violins and cellos, and tuning instruments I'd never seen before. Their vibrations swirled together into the air, filling Lewisohn Stadium with a whirlwind of joyful sound.

Before the stage were long curving rows of concrete steps. And behind the steps was a great wall lined with huge stone columns that looked exactly like the ones in *Demetrius and the Gladiator*, a movie I'd just seen about ancient Rome.

"We'd better get to our seats," my father said.

Taking my hand, he began climbing the stairway, sitting at last in the row just before the columns.

❖

A man with wavy white hair strode onto the stage, and the audience broke into a round of applause. Now he tapped the music stand with his baton, and the stadium hushed.

"He's the conductor," my father whispered in my ear. "They're all waiting for his signal to begin."

The conductor looked to the left, and then to the right. Violinists and cellists leaned forward on their chairs, holding their bows at the ready. The white-haired man raised both his hands, and like honey flowing from a jar, a quiet melody filled the stadium.

Now I, too, was at the edge of my seat.

The conductor's body began swaying from side to

side. Suddenly, his mop of neatly combed hair was flying about him. He thrust his baton to the right, calling to the trumpets, as a haunting refrain rose above the cellos.

A moment later, the conductor beckoned, and like a troupe of tiny ballerinas, the flutes waltzed into the symphony. Their high, sprightly melodies darted above the others in a dance of exultation. Now they were joined by a gaggle of instruments, as the full voice of the orchestra echoed through the air.

As I sat there, images flooded into my brain.

With the blast of a single trumpet, a herd of

The Three Musicians
Bruce Waldman
Etching

winged stallions dashed through the stream of a mystical forest. Cymbals crashed, sending droplets of white mist spraying from their hooves. The tympani boomed, and the horses galloped into a clearing, flapped their wings, and soared into the sky.

The stallions rose higher and higher, vanishing behind the clouds, and the music turned to color. Flutes were a silvery blue. Cellos produced waves of purple velvet. Trumpet blasts turned to orange flame. I floated on a rainbow river, passing beneath waterfalls of light.

❖

During the intermission my father left, and returned with one of my favorites: a creamsicle cup of vanilla ice cream and orange ices. I sat slurping it on a flat wooden spoon, waiting for the orchestra to return. Then the musicians started walking out onto the stage, took their seats, and the conductor returned to thunderous applause. When the audience quieted, he raised his baton once again, and I slid to the edge of my seat. Within moments, I was back in the mythical forest.

"It's the second symphony of a man from Finland," my father whispered. "It's about the beautiful pine forests he knew so well."

His words washed over me like morning sunlight, and as my father continued whispering in my ear, telling me about the life and music of composer Jean Sibelius, I basked in the soothing tones of a voice I had never heard before. It was as if he had removed a shadowy mask, revealing the face of a gentle and loving man who had previously lived in darkness.

Several weeks after that first concert, he brought me to a place called Carnegie Hall, where we sat and listened to Harry Belafonte singing story-songs of bananas, sailing ships, and brown-skinned maidens from the Carribean.

But that was just the beginning.

In the coming months, my father introduced me to a section of the city that was different from anything I'd seen before, a place whose parks and alleyways were filled with long-haired poets and intellectuals — "Beatniks" as he called them. It was a place teeming with sidewalk cafes, tree-lined streets, and little theaters jammed with the sounds of jazz and folk music. My father called it "The Village," Greenwich Village. And it was there, in the coffee houses beneath the sidewalks, that he introduced me to the music of Josh White, the Weavers, Paul Robeson, and Woody Guthrie.

◦∴❖∵◦

During those years, my parents continued to battle through the nights, but for me, something was forever changed.

For though my father still evoked images of the truant officer when he was enraged, his threats began to resemble hollow buildings made of mist, structures whose walls were created, not of steel or stone, but of feathers, clouds, and wisps of wind.

For I had heard the music of his kind and loving voice, and seen the sweet and gentle man behind the mask.

And I was never terrified again.

Brother Sun, Sister Moon
Neil Waldman
Oil on linen

Chapter Seventeen

Richie

༄M̲y father and I seemed to grow closer with each passing day. We'd created a new ritual: strolling together in the evenings after dinner along the tree-lined sidewalks of Wilson Avenue, shmoozing about folk music, art, and stickball. It was clear to me that we were making up for lost time, getting to know each other at last, finally becoming what we'd actually been all along: a father and his son.

But there were other things that weren't going so smoothly.

I was a fifth-grader now, class 5A to be exact, and though it made me quite uncomfortable, I was beginning to feel a bit stifled by my mother. She always seemed to be hovering over me, and though I never meant to hurt her, I started spending my afternoons and weekends playing stickball. I'd tried introducing her to a couple of my teammates, but when I brought them home after our games, she always made it clear that she didn't like having them in the house.

"Why don't you bring some nicer, better-behaved boys home?" she'd say.

Then, on a chilly spring evening, the uncomfortable situation reached a boiling point when Richie Greenberg, my closest buddy and fellow stickball player, took me exploring along the moss-covered banks of the Bronx River.

⌣∴❖∴⌣

It happened on a Friday afternoon.

Mrs. Frischmann (known to us as "Ole Miss Fishcakes" because her breath smelled like rotten gefilte fish) passed out our weekend homework sheets the way she always did, just as the dismissal bell started ringing.

"Let's get outa here!" Richie shouted as we flew down three flights of stairs and charged out onto—you guessed it—*Fish* Avenue!

Leaving our books in his mother's apartment, we started sprinting along the sidewalks of Boston Road, dodging little kids and ladies pushing baby carriages. We darted past John's Bargain Store and The Melba, our neighborhood movie house, and cruised into a new ice-cream parlor called Crystal Creme, where we guzzled a lime rickey with two straws. Then we turned onto

Gunhill Road, passed beneath the blue shadows of the
elevated subway, and scampered down onto the wooded
banks of the Bronx River.

Perched high above the muddy stream on the
spreading branches of a big old maple, we watched the
chocolate water flowing beneath us. Pulling out packs
of baseball cards, we stuffed sticks of bubble gum into
out mouths as we considered the adventures that might
come our way over the weekend.

"Hey, Neil-man, wanna take a subway ride to the
Stadium?" Richie asked. "I'm pretty sure the Yanks are
playing a twin bill on Sunday."

*Sounds cool. But what about going to Ebbets Field
instead. The Dodgers are playing the 'Jints.*

"You still hot on 'dem bums?"

Yup. Sure am.

"Well, maybe we should flip a coin."

·:❖:·

Richie and I sat up in that tree for hours, debat-
ing the plusses and minuses of New York's three great
centerfielders as the unconsidered sky turned brilliant
orange. Then, like a checkerboard of glowing rectan-
gles, lights started flickering on in apartment after
apartment until the Bronx skyline shimmered. Still,
neither Richie nor I took notice. By the time the moon
floated over the rooftops, we still hadn't agreed on

whether Mickey Mantle, Willie Mays, or Duke Snider was the greatest centerfielder in New York.

Then, I glanced at my watch.

Holy Toledo! It's six-thirty!

We jumped down from the tree and began running along the riverbank. Then, as we neared Gunhill Road, Richie spotted a rubber ball floating between some bottles and crates among the ripples.

"It's a Spauldine!" he shouted. "I've gotta have it!"

He leaned out over the river, but the ball was just beyond his grasp. Inching closer to the water's edge, he stretched out and swiped at it. As the ball bobbed away in the current, Richie started swaying back and forth. Unable to regain his balance, he lunged at an overhanging branch and fell in. Within a split second, Richie was up to his armpits in the garbage-infested waters.

"It's freezin' in here!" he cried out.

I managed to pull my buddy out, but as we started walking home, Richie began to shiver.

Let's stop at my house. We should get you out of those wet clothes as soon as we can.

"Aw right," Richie said between shivers.

Five minutes later, we ran up onto the front stoop, and there, standing like an icy statue, was my mother. Her arms looked like jagged triangles, elbows sticking out from both sides, with both fists clenched at her hips.

"Where have you been!" she demanded. "I've been worried sick about you!"

Sorry. But Richie's all wet. Can he come in and . . .

"No! He may not!" she barked, pushing the door open. "Now, get inside this minute!"

⌁ ❖ ⌁

I suffered through the weekend, stewing in that mixture of anger, guilt, and embarrassment that so many kids have to endure in silence. But my discomfort was to be short-lived, for as soon as we trotted out onto the stickball field on Monday afternoon, those dreaded feelings evaporated with the opening pitch.

Richie and I would remain best buddies until my family moved from the Bronx two years later. During those times, we joined and quit the Cub Scouts together, became blood brothers, and shared secret stories about the girlfriends we dreamed of. And it was at his mom's place, on a Tuesday afternoon in December, that Richie taught me my first dirty word.

"Wait till you get an earful of what I just heard!" Richie said, closing the bedroom door behind him. "Bobby Sampson just let me in on it! An honest-to-God cuss word, exactly like the ones the geezers use!"

I was shocked.

Grown-ups don't use curse words!

"Yuh kiddin' me, right?"
Richie leaned over and stared straight into my eyes.
"Listen up, Neil-man. Bobby heard his ole man usin' this very word last night!"

Really?

"Yuh got my word on it."

OK. . . . So anyway, what is it?

"Bitch."

Well, what does . . . I mean, what is a . . . bitch?

Now Richie licked his lips, glanced to the left and right, and put a hand on my shoulder.

"If yuh really wanna know the God's honest truth, it's a foul-smellin', vomit-drippin', greasy pig of a woman!"

⌒❖⌒

Two days later I was in the back alleyway, on the swings with Brucie and Bryna, when I cupped my hands and yelled toward the house.

Hey, Maaa!

The kitchen window slid open, and our mother leaned out.

"What is it?" she called to me.

You're a bitch!

Within seconds, she was out in the alleyway.

"Come with me, Neil," she said in a stern voice, taking my hand. She led me inside and sat me down on the living-room couch.

"Do you know what that word means?" she asked.

Yes. It means . . . a nice lady.

"No," she answered. "That's not what it means at all. You should know that a bitch is actually a female dog, but the way it's used in this culture, well, it's an angry curse word, used by uncultured, uneducated people. Someone as creative and intelligent as you should never use it again."

I'm real sorry.

"That's perfectly all right," she said quietly. "Now, you may go back outside."

❖

Though I'd worried that my mother would match my fury with a wilder fury of her own, her calm and rational response made a lasting impression on me. In later years, as I went through sixth, seventh, and eighth grades, I would be exposed to many words far more vulgar than that one, but I chose never to use any of them, even among stickball players, classmates, and friends.

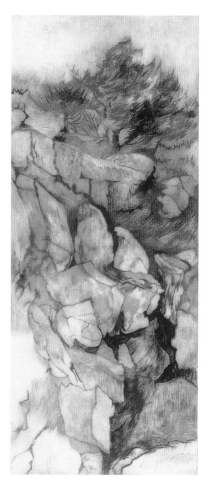

Acadian Landscape I
Jean Morris
Etching

Acadian Landscape II
Jean Morris
Etching

Chapter Eighteen

The Petrie Dish

᠁Summer turned to winter and back into summer. Though I continued playing stickball, I now spent most of my free time drawing and painting. I sketched while riding on buses, in the Nash Rambler, and on the subway. I painted before breakfast, after dinner, and on weekends. I even painted instead of doing my homework.

And an incredible thing began to happen. My artwork got better and better!

Without even trying, I was learning—learning to paint from memories of great stickball games. Learning to draw leaping outfielders and sliding base runners, and learning to sketch my newest favorites: cave men, mythological creatures, and dinosaurs. It seemed remarkable to me that while experiencing so

Creatures
Neil Waldman (age 11)
Watercolor and felt pen

much pleasure I was becoming a better artist, without even trying.

And then I learned something else.

When my parents were locked in combat, I could blot out their voices by taking out my pencils and sketchpad, and concentrating on a drawing. The more I learned to focus my attention on my artwork, the quieter their voices became. And every once in a while, when I managed to lose myself totally in a drawing, their voices would disappear completely.

❧ ❖ ❦

On a Saturday morning, Brucie, Bryna, David, and I sat on the living-room floor, sculpting with pipe cleaners, tin foil, and modeling clay. Beyond the open doorway, our parents sat opposite each other, exchanging hostile whispers across the kitchen table. Slowly, the volume increased, as staccato barbs caromed into the living room. I looked up and saw that my brothers and sister were staring at our parents, whose faces were red with rage, their eyes piercing each other like sharpened swords.

I looked down at my pipe-cleaner "Tyrannosaurus," and crushed it between my fingers. Now my parents' voices were exploding in my brain. Suddenly, I sprang to my feet and stood facing them.

I can't stand it anymore! Just l e a v e   m e   a l o n e ! I'm going to my room!

With my stomach quaking and fists clenched at my sides, I stomped up the stairs and slammed the bedroom door. Dropping onto a chair, my mind went numb as I sat there trembling beneath the black waves of a pain-filled ocean.

Then, from somewhere far away, I remembered my mother's book. My old hero Vincent van Gogh gently reached out and directed my gaze to the box of colored pencils on my desk.

Before I realized it, I was drawing.

I sketched two twisting cypress trees and a swollen river that raged between them. Beyond the trees, I drew a knight on horseback slaying a two-headed dragon. Above the horizon, I summoned wave after wave of thunderclouds rumbling across the blackening skies. And in the upper right-hand corner, I sketched a thin ray of sunlight that shone all the way across the page, cutting through the clouds and glinting off the knight's iron helmet.

Suddenly, there was a knocking at the door, and Brucie poked his head into the bedroom.

"Could I draw with you?" he asked.

Sure.

He pulled a chair up next to mine, took out his crayons, and started drawing a cowboy on a pinto pony. I returned to my drawing, and we worked together for hours.

❖

Weeks passed, and our studio quietly shifted from the living-room floor to the desktops of our bedroom. Whenever I sensed the beginnings of an argument between our parents, I'd gesture to Brucie, and we'd escape to our hideaway.

One day, Bryna knocked on the door and asked if she could join us. And two or three years after that, David was accepted into our secret society.

So began a loving chapter in the lives of the Waldman children. We retreated often to our bedroom hideaway, spending those turbulent days together. In our sheltered haven, unbearable burdens were lifted from our shoulders as wild colors flowed from our brushes onto sheets of snow-white paper.

Years later, I came to think of our childhood home as "The Petrie Dish," recognizing that it had been an environment where artists would have no choice but to blossom. Our parents' love of and support for the arts had provided us with an escape route from the stormy seas into which we'd been cast.

For art was our lifeboat.

The Red Line
Neil Waldman
Oil on canvas

On the shores of that terrible ocean lay a land of soothing sunshine, where one could bask in the sweet worlds of unreality.

Once I discovered that magical land and inhaled its perfume, I would not be denied. After crossing that sickening sea for the last time, I was fated to follow the fragrances that had penetrated the castle walls of my heart—and I knew that I would always follow them—to the ends of the earth if need be.

And in this I was not alone.

For Brucie, Bryna, and David had also inhaled the perfume.

It's no coincidence that of the four of us, three grew up to become artists.

Today, Brucie's etchings and monoprints are included in the permanent collections of the Metropolitan Museum of Art in New York City and the Library of Congress/Smithsonian Institution in Washington, D.C. His works have been exhibited in Lincoln Center in New York and City Hall in Paris. He teaches printmaking at the School of Visual Arts and drawing at the Westchester Art Workshop. Bruce has created many illustrations for books and magazines and is a director of the New York Society of Etchers.

Bryna worked in London for several years, creating many children's books for Cambridge University Press. She then returned home to illustrate *Anansi Finds a Fool* by Verna Aardema and several other American picture books. Bryna is also a teacher, guitarist, and folk singer.

Self-Portrait
Bryna Waldman
Pen and ink

I am a landscape painter, writer, illustrator, and teacher. I've designed postage stamps for thirteen nations. My books have received the Christopher Award, the National Jewish Book Award, the A.L.A. Notable Award, and the Parents' Choice Award, among others. My book-jacket illustrations have appeared on the covers of seven Newbery Award winners, including *A Fine White Dust* by Cynthia Rylant and *Hatchet* by Gary Paulsen. Along with Brucie, I teach watercolor painting at the Westchester Art Workshop.

Only David has chosen a life outside the visual arts, working as a teacher and spiritual healer in Oregon.

Postage Stamp Designs
Neil Waldman
Acrylic on board

Afterimage

❧ I'm speaking in an auditorium packed with ninth- and tenth-graders, telling stories of my childhood years in the Bronx, when a girl in one of the back rows stands up, raises her hand, and asks this question.

"Could you tell us how you became a real artist?"

What do you mean, a real artist?

"You know," she counters. "Someone who gets paid for it!"

I stop to reflect for a moment, and as I scan the room, my mind flashes to a cherished bookshelf in my studio. There, stacked against one another, are seven official-looking journals with brown leather covers, five spiral sketchbooks, a cardboard folder stuffed with drawings, and my very first journal, an old speckled black-and-white composition book from Miss Bogel's first-grade class.

I remember the first three words I wrote in that book.

I am sad.

I consider those words, remembering how writing and rereading them helped me to get through the pain I was living with. I now recognize that my life as a writer began the moment I put them down on paper.

Sketchbook Page
Bruce Waldman
Charcoal pencil

Then, like a great wave, Vincent's colors come flooding into my brain: brilliant blues, swirling purples, vibrating aquas and indigos, and I smile.

I reflect on those remarkable colors, washing over me again and again during the days of my childhood.

I remember the portrait that hung for years on my bedroom wall, and recognize that it was Vincent's extraordinary sense of color and his love of humanity that touched my soul.

Though he wasn't able to save himself, the master's paintings humbled and inspired me, giving me the strength I needed to overcome life's obstacles. Like a guardian angel, Vincent carried me out of the shadows, down sunlit pathways, into the healing waters of my imagination.

I look out at the eager faces that fill the auditorium.

They're all so young . . . thirteen, fourteen, fifteen years old . . . young minds that don't forget a single thing.

But I know now that it won't always be that way. After a person turns thirty, forty, and then fifty, his memory starts to slip. I know that I've been fortunate. For the things I recorded on paper will never be lost. When I reread an old journal entry or look at an early drawing, floods of memory often come back to me. Sometimes a sentence or a slash of color will bring back an entire episode.

As I've grown older, more and more of my books are based on things I recorded in my journals and sketchpads. I know now that many of my books would never have come into being if I hadn't drawn or written things down when I was young.

But that's not all.

You see, something else happened because I kept sketchbooks and journals.

Sketchbook Page
Neil Waldman
Pen and ink

Without realizing it, I gradually honed the crafts of writing, drawing, and painting. Day after day, week after week, year after year, I developed the skills necessary to become a *real* artist. Like so many things in life, when you do something over and over again, you usually get better at it.

I turn to the young girl at the back of the auditorium, take in a deep breath, and begin speaking.

Sketchbooks and journals are the streetlamps that illuminate the artist's journey. . . .